Professional Development in the
Lifelong Learning Sector

Maintaining Your Licence
to Practise

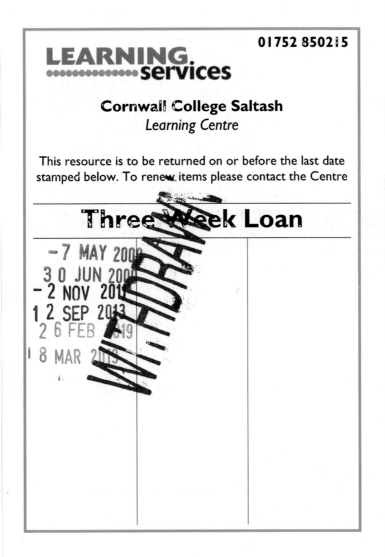

Professional Development in the
Lifelong Learning Sector

Maintaining Your Licence to Practise

 Jeanne Hitching

LearningMatters

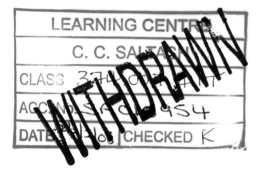
First published in 2008 by Learning Matters Ltd.

© 2008 Jeanne Hitching

British Library Cataloguing in Publication Data
A CIP record for this book is available from the British Library.

ISBN: 978 1 84445 137 1

The right of Jeanne Hitching to be identified as author of this work
has been asserted by her in accordance with the Copyright,
Design and Patents Act 1998

Cover design by Topics – The Creative Partnership
Project management by Deer Park Productions, Tavistock, Devon
Typeset by Pantek Arts Ltd, Maidstone, Kent
Printed and bound in Great Britain by Cromwell Press Ltd, Trowbridge, Wiltshire

Learning Matters Ltd
33 Southernhay East
Exeter EX1 1NX
Tel: 01392 215560
info@learningmatters.co.uk
www.learningmatters.co.uk

Contents

Acknowledgements

I would like to thank Lee Davies for his support whilst I was writing this book and for supplying the foreword.

I would also like to thank my husband David and daughters Jo and Zoe who saw to it that I sometimes took a break from writing and got on with life.

Foreword

Often, when I speak at conferences or meet with colleagues in colleges and other learning providers, I am asked the 'why' question. Why is CPD important? When I first responded to that question I drew heavily on something David Blunkett said in 2000, addressing the continuing professional development of teachers in our schools:

> *Nobody expects a doctor, accountant or lawyer to rely for decades solely on the knowledge, understanding and approach which was available at the time when they began their career. Good professionals are engaged in a journey of self-improvement, always ready to reflect on their own practice in the light of other approaches and to contribute to the development of others by sharing their best practice and insights. They learn from what works.* [1]

I think that still stands up as a rationale for the importance of CPD; but I became concerned that it perpetuates the belief that extrinsic drivers are of greatest importance; CPD is important because government/employers/ professional bodies tell us it is. I wanted something more abstract, something that teachers could connect with, something that starts to unravel the intrinsic motivation that is at the heart of professional development. More by accident than design I stumbled across this quotation, taken from *The Restaurant at the End of the Universe* by Douglas Adams:

> *There is a theory which states that if ever anyone discovers exactly what the Universe is for and why it is here, it will instantly disappear and be replaced by something even more bizarre and inexplicable. There is another theory which states that this has already happened.* [2]

This works for me in the following way; substitute '*teaching*' for '*the Universe*' and you have the prime, intrinsic reason why CPD is important for each and every teacher. Reflecting back on my own 20-year teaching career, whenever I felt that I was in command of my teaching universe something would change to alter that steady state. City & Guilds qualifications became NVQ; classes of predominately adult learners became 16–18 year-old youth trainees, became 14–16 year-old school pupils; not to mention the impact of external influences such as inspection and policy initiatives.

As a teacher, CPD is the only way I can maintain the currency of my professional practice, ensuring I am the best subject specialist I can be and that I am fully equipped in terms of the skills and knowledge I need as a teacher. I am really excited by the current level of attention that *teacher professionalism* is receiving, both in terms of the emerging reform agenda leading to a regulated workforce and the Institute for Learning advocacy of *dual professionalism* within a teacher-centric model of CPD. I firmly believe we have the opportunity to return teacher professionalism to the top of the educational agenda, after all: what is self-regulation if it is not the regulation of professionalism through a community of practice?

Having responded to the *'why'* question I am usually confronted with the *'what'* conundrum. What counts as CPD? Well, through reading this book and the extensive literature that exists around professional development, you will discover that there is no single answer. Effective CPD is highly personalised with critical reflection leading us to consider what we do well, what we do less well and how we develop both for the benefit of ourselves and our learners. There can be no list of 'dos and dont's', all that matters is that I identify development activities that respond to the needs of my teaching practice as I understand it today.

Let me offer you another analogy, only this time comparing CPD to Alice's travels in Wonderland:

> *'Cheshire Puss,' she began, rather timidly, as she did not at all know whether it would like the name: however, it only grinned a little wider. 'Come, it's pleased so far,' thought Alice, and she went on. 'Would you tell me, please, which way I ought to go from here?'*
>
> *'That depends a good deal on where you want to get to,' said the Cat.*
>
> *'I don't much care where –' said Alice.*
>
> *'Then it doesn't matter which way you go,' said the Cat.*
>
> *'– so long as I get SOMEWHERE,' Alice added as an explanation.*
>
> *'Oh, you're sure to do that,' said the Cat, 'if you only walk long enough.'* [3]

For me, this sums up continuing professional development. Very often we start from a position of not knowing where we will end up; we simply identify something about our professional practice we want to improve. I might want to use the internet in new and different ways in my teaching; that need might lead me to a taster session in e-learning; in turn I may look to work towards a formal qualification in ICT. Where I end up isn't that important, what I learn along the way and my ability to reflect that in my approach to teaching and learning are.

Whatever you do, enjoy your journey!

Lee Davies
Operations Manager

The Institute for Learning

References

(1) Department for Education and Employment (2000) *Professional Development: Support for Teaching and Learning.* London: HMSO.

(2) Adams, D. (1980) *The Restaurant at the End of the Universe.* London: Pan Books.

(3) Carroll, L. (1865) *Alice's Adventures in Wonderland.*

Introduction

The post-compulsory education and training sector (PCET) has long been recognised for the critical role it plays in meeting the needs of the economy through the education, training and ongoing development of the workforce in the UK.

As the teachers, trainers and tutors working in the sector, you are drawn from diverse backgrounds. An increasing number of you are graduates, and whether you are or not, the majority of you have a high level of specialist vocational skill and a wealth of industrial experience to bring to the learning environment.

Your role in the post-compulsory education world is an increasingly complex one. Not only are you expected to train the workforce of today and tomorrow in the latest technology and skills, you must also be permanently several steps ahead of rapidly changing government priorities whilst maintaining an overview of relevant legislation and operating within the guidelines of your own institution.

Quite apart from that, as practitioners in the sector, you operate by necessity within the context of dual professionalism. Your academic and vocational expertise in the main has been gained first and later, quite often while working in the sector, your subject knowledge and skills are supplemented with a teacher training qualification which recognises your specific practitioner skills.

relevant

For many years, teaching and learning capabilities were viewed as having a lower priority than industrial experience and subject knowledge and, in that climate, many lecturers got by with minimal support in developing their classroom skills. Indeed, many lecturers who taught part-time whilst retaining a foothold in their vocational area would have baulked at being told how to teach, arguing that their subject knowledge and experience in 'the real world' was all that was required. By degrees that situation has moved from one where a teaching qualification was rare, to one where it was advisable, but not compulsory, to one where it will be required as condition to teach. Furthermore, qualifying as a teacher in the sector will be just the beginning of a career-long undertaking in terms of professional development.

From late 2007, Qualified Teacher Learning and Skills (QTLS) will be conferred on those in the sector satisfactorily completing an approved teacher training course. The award will come from the Institute for Learning (IfL) (www.ifl.ac.uk). The Institute for Learning has played a central role in the reform of initial teacher training and professional development for the post-compulsory sector through the implementation of the agenda highlighted in *Equipping our Teachers for the Future* (DfES, November 2004).

The outcome has been the development of a new professional identity for practitioners that not only embodies a set of shared values and expectations about conduct and practice but also identifies a career-long commitment to professional development in order to maintain good standing. This overt commitment to continuing professional development (CPD) has become a key feature of the reform, not least because of the impact it will have on every individual and institution concerned with post-compulsory education and training.

The section of the reform relating to the new Licence to Practise means that every practitioner working in the sector will need to ensure from 2007 that they can provide regular, clear evidence to the Institute for Learning that they have undertaken some kind of professional development commensurate with the level of their role and responsibilities. They will be asked to file a return to the IfL approximately once a year from the date of their registration to that effect, together with evidence of the developments undertaken and reflection on the process or processes involved.

This book has been written to:

- provide you, the reader, with some background and context for the introduction of the Licence to Practise and the introduction of a continuing professional development tariff from 2007;
- outline the role of the Institute for Learning in the process;
- offer a range of development activities that you could undertake as all or part of your regular CPD tariff for the Institute for Learning;
- outline the importance of the function of reflection in the CPD process;
- provide you with some tools to reflect on different types of development activities;
- extend the debate about the nature and purpose of continuing professional development for practitioners in the sector.

This book has been written for:

- any of you, in any part of the sector, who want to be informed about the role and function of the Institute for Learning and what the changes starting in 2007 mean for you and your practice;
- anyone, in any part of the sector, who wants to play a key role in participating in their own professional development;
- workforce development professionals in the Lifelong Learning sector who design and deliver aspects of staff training;
- sector line managers responsible for appraisal and or performance review;
- mentors supporting colleague development.

How to get the best from this book

There is not one way and one way only to use this book. Some people like to start at the beginning and systematically work their way through, chapter by chapter. Others prefer to take a more 'pick and mix' approach, dipping randomly into chapters and doing piecemeal activities that appeal at the time. Some people need to understand the context of any change or initiative before getting involved in anything practical. Others are keen to launch into the activities without worrying too much about the processes that lead up to their creation. You will know how you like to work, though it may useful to say that:

- if you are the linear, systematic type and prefer to work through the book in the 'right order' you may benefit in terms of perspective from 'skimming' the chapters first to get an overview before you start. This way, you will appreciate the bigger picture and what is to come as well as what you are reading now;

- if you tend to read a book from the middle outwards and only look properly at the bits that appeal at that moment, you too might benefit from a better idea of the overall content and context of the book. Try reading the introduction that outlines the content of each chapter and ask yourself after reading each chapter outline to note at least two reasons why what it has to say could be an advantage for you to know;

- if you are the theoretical type and always find yourself seeking out some context before you can deal with anything practical, you will no doubt appreciate the way this book is set out because it does follow that format. Ultimately though, this book is about practical strategies designed to demonstrate professional development. So, the 'doing element' needs to be given equal billing with the theoretical;

- some people are very happy to launch themselves into anything practical. They tend to be more concerned with the 'what' and less concerned with the 'why' of any task. Whilst this may be a useful state of mind to have in some situations, it may also lead to a less critically aware approach to any outcomes. Such folk will want to get straight down to the development activities because they are there rather than because any particular one stands out as a professionally desirable undertaking. As a result, when it comes to the reflective element of the activity, they may struggle to really engage. If you think you might be a bit like this, try to step back and think carefully before you select and start an activity for your CPD. You might also consider beginning with the activities outlined in Chapter 4 since quite a number of them in this section have a particular focus on developing critical self-awareness. An alternative would be to discuss your proposed choice of development activity with a trusted colleague or mentor. Having to explain your choice to someone else is a useful aid to kick-start the reflective process.

Chapter content

For readers who appreciate context, Chapter 1 provides some recent background to the development of the QTLS and ATLS qualifications (Qualified Teacher Learning and Skills and Associate Teacher Learning and Skills) and the introduction of a Licence to Practise for all of you working as practitioners in the sector. It also outlines what these reforms mean, in practical terms, for all practitioners, thus alerting managers and staff developers to some key in-house development opportunities.

This chapter is also designed to offer you a closer focus on the processes of the continuing professional development cycle and how it will be likely to function at an institutional and personal level. Much of the content in this chapter has come about as the result of discussions with practitioners and staff developers working in the sector and addresses a series of questions that have arisen frequently enough to indicate a section of their own. So it covers the nature of the CPD process with the IfL, the nature of the links between the new teacher standards and the CPD process, the CPD tariff, registering with the IfL and using the IfL website to participate in and record individual development activities. It also explains how the quality aspects of the CPD process are likely to be measured and managed by the IfL to ensure consistency in standards.

By this point you will probably observe that there is a noticeable emphasis from the IfL on the requirement for reflection from practitioners. Indeed, evidence of real engagement with reflective practice as a tool for developing professional skills and knowledge will be the key to maintaining the licence to practise. Chapter 2 both examines the need for reflection as part of professional behaviour and offers some discussion about how certain theories and models of reflection could be turned into practical and useful tools to aid the sort of reflection that can have real impact on practice and satisfy the IfL at the same time. Some further examples of simple tools that could be used to aid reflective thinking and behaviour are offered in this chapter. They address such issues as how to ask reflective questions, how to identify and model excellence and the difference between keeping a general diary and writing reflectively.

Chapter 3 precludes the beginning of the section covering the development activities by addressing some issues that it would be useful to be clear about before getting started. For example, what counts as CPD from the IfL perspective? How can practitioners and staff developers select a development activity or set of activities that are relevant and meaningful both to those undertaking them and to the IfL? This chapter aims to address those points.

This section also covers useful ways to maximise learning and reflection potential from external training and in-house development activities by suggesting some reflective approaches that could be applied to meet the CPD requirements of the IfL tariff. Some thoughts are also offered about how to harness appraisal and/or performance review to identify areas of professional interest and training need.

It seemed important to include some advice on the sort of language and style it would be useful to adopt when writing up development activities and reflections, so I have done this here together with some support with issues around referencing and plagiarism.

Finally, this chapter discusses the nature of the evidence that the IfL will want to see and advises you what to do with the supplementary material you will need to retain for IfL sampling and quality assurance. The main aim of this chapter then is to encourage all of you to maximise your continuing professional development potential by engaging with your CPD activities in the full knowledge of what you have to do, and the most efficient and rewarding way of going about it.

Chapters 4, 5 and 6 move into the more practical aspects of this book by offering you a number of different structured development activities, any of which could be used as evidence of continuing professional development in your annual return to the Institute for Learning. They are divided into two main themes to reflect the model of dual professionalism that underpins teaching in the post-compulsory sector.

The first theme covers professional values, professional behaviour and the development of your specialist knowledge and pedagogy.

The second theme addresses the elements of your practice more directly related to planning, delivering, supporting and assessing learning.

In every case, a link is made between each activity and the domains A–F as they are set out in the new teacher standards. This will enable you to cross-reference your development activities with any other institutional strategic aims and enable consistency in professional development tracking as the process develops. The activities themselves are designed to have a connection to your current professional experience and by investigating and reflecting on related elements, you will be able to 'grow your own practice' in response to your personal career aims as well as meet the needs of your employer and the sector. This approach to continuing professional development, located within a culture of improvement and supported by reflection, suggests a connection with experiential learning and certain models of action research, both of which have a long pedigree in classroom-based educational research.

In many ways, the CPD process will enable you to systematise and formalise much of the reflection and innovation already happening in your learning environment. Better still, there will be the potential to share your discoveries via the IfL website and collaborate with fellow practitioners along the way.

Finally, for those who relish the thought of exploring the links between theory and practice, you have the opportunity here to do just that as part of your reflection. For many of you though, the reflection may centre more on the impact your activity and outcomes have had on your practice. Either way, reflection and even *reflection about reflection* will emerge as a key feature of any development activity you elect to undertake as part of your professional development.

1. Professionalism in context

CHAPTER OBJECTIVES

This chapter is designed to:

- outline the key structures and functions introduced by the Institute for Learning in relation to the QTLS, ATLS and the continuing professional development process;

- outline the principles underpinning the CPD model;

- address the most frequently asked questions about how the CPD process will work;

- suggest strategies you could adopt to get into the professional development mindset.

The post-compulsory education and training sector is a model of dynamic complexity. Teachers, trainers and tutors operate out of further education colleges, higher education establishments, work-based learning centres, community and outreach provision and prison education. All of you working in such roles play a critical part in shaping the current and future workforce and in the health and development of the economy at almost every level. Many of you will have entered teaching through non-traditional routes, bringing a range of vocational skills and industrial experience to the learning environment. Others will be graduates and postgraduates. All of you are working in this sector because you have specialist knowledge and skills that can contribute to the growth of the economy and the well-being of those who depend on it.

Dual professionalism and the new QTLS

There are very few generalist practitioners in this sector. The majority of you have developed expertise in one or more distinct and specialist areas. These areas range across the academic, business, commercial and industrial worlds and deliver learning at many different levels of ability. Given that your teaching will potentially produce the national wealth of tomorrow, your professional expertise needs to remain current; no easy undertaking when technologies are developing so rapidly. Furthermore, in order to pass those skills on to others effectively, training how to teach is now considered to have an equal priority with subject specialism.

From September 2007, either Associate Teacher Learning and Skills (ATLS), or Qualified Teacher Learning and Skills (QTLS) status, granted by the Institute for Learning, will underpin the professional identity of teachers in the sector and complement subject specialist skills. Those of you already holding a teaching qualification (for example, a certificate of education or postgraduate certificate of education) will be able to have your existing qualifications recognised, providing they match certain criteria, to avoid repetition of training.

Underlying principles of the professional development model

In 2006, the Institute for Learning in its role as the professional body for practitioners in post-compulsory education and training, produced a response to the Further Education White Paper, *Raising Skills, Improving Life-Chances*. In it they welcomed the government plan to deliver significant improvements to teaching and learning for post-compulsory education.

As part of that change, the IfL has played a leading role in the reform of initial teacher training and developing the professionalisation of the sector. In particular this has meant the creation of a career-long commitment to professional growth that emerges from the point QTLS or ATLS is achieved. The continuing professional development model is linked firmly to the Licence to Practise and thus places an obligation on all teachers to engage with regular and meaningful professional development in order to remain in good standing as a licensed practitioner.

In putting together the requirements and criteria for professional development for practitioners, the IfL has been careful to ensure that the model chosen reflects those of comparable professional bodies. It is unlikely that anyone has ever questioned that doctors, nurses and other professional medical practitioners should continually update and refresh their skills. Their knowledge and skills must remain current in order for them to continue safely and reliably in practice. Similar underlying principles apply in the legal profession. So, when you look at the underpinning philosophy and operating principles supporting the introduction of CPD into post-compulsory teaching, you can see that at heart it has come about to support and reinforce the broadening and deepening of professional behaviour and provide a clear structure in which that continuous process can operate.

In a general sense, the sector as a whole will clearly benefit from such a structure, but it is also clear that a system that supports the entitlement to continuing professional development will also, over time, increase career choices and opportunities and promote greater autonomy for individual practitioners.

The key principles of the Institution for Learning CPD model are that:

- professional development is a continuous process that will add value throughout your career;
- professional development is most effective when used in conjunction with reflection – this enables you to truly evaluate the impact of any training on all aspects of your practice;

- what is learned and how it is incorporated into your practice is more important than the time it takes you to do it;
- you are at the centre of the process – it means taking responsibility for reflecting on and identifying your own development needs;
- your professional development plan should set out your development needs, show measurable outcomes, link to your teaching context and resonate with employer objectives;
- your professional development should include a range of activities over time that address both your subject specialist area and your teaching and learning role;
- there needs to be a balance over time of formal and informal development activities;
- professional development works best when integrated with your work role.

Leading on from this, the model for the process of continuing professional development set by the Institute for Learning has six distinct steps for each of you to undertake annually. Details of this process will appear on the IfL website to guide you (www.ifl.ac.uk) but the main features of the process are as follows:

Annual CPD procedure

- **Step one**: Reflect on your professional practice to date.
- **Step two**: Carry out a gap analysis to identify development needs.
- **Step three**: Create your professional development plan.
- **Step four**: Undertake professional development activities.
- **Step five**: Reflect on the impact professional development has had on your practice.
- **Step six**: Complete your professional development record and return it to the IfL either through the website or by post.

If you plan to undertake several smaller development activities or projects over any 12-month period, you will need to carry out this simple six-step plan for each one.

Remaining in good standing

In addition to your annual CPD activities and reflection, in order to remain in good standing with the Institute for Learning and maintain your licence to practise, you will need to:

- ensure that your membership subscription to the IfL is paid up in full on an annual basis;
- meet the requirements of the IfL for recording your CPD activities via the online portal or other approved manner;
- comply with the terms of the code of professional values and practice as set out by the IfL.

Sampling CPD and quality assurance

Your Licence to Practise will be renewed on an annual basis by the Institute for Learning. They will periodically review the data entered against each member and raise an 'alert' for anyone perceived at risk of failing to comply with CPD criteria. In such a case, you would be offered support to meet the requirements to remain in good standing.

The Institute for Learning will also sample a range of evidence from the online professional development records annually using a stratified sample to increase the validity and reliability of the process. If your annual return is selected for sampling, you will be asked to provide evidence of the CPD activities you have carried out in the previous 12 months. This evidence may be examined remotely with the IfL paying the cost of postage or, in some cases, arrangements might be made to sample your work during a visit to your institution. The producers of examples of best practice will be encouraged to share their ideas with members via the online community.

Key questions

Although there is a significant amount of information about the new system for CPD in the public arena (see www.ifl.ac.uk and www.lluk.ac.uk), there are a number of issues and questions that tend to be raised in current discussions about the nature of continuing professional development and the impact the new requirements will have on practitioners. Below are 12 of the most frequently posed. If the responses here do not solve your particular problem, or answer the question for your particular case, the Institute for Learning will be able to help you. The website carries a lot of information, including telephone numbers for those of you who prefer to make direct contact.

Why do I have to do CPD?

You play a critical role in the training and development of the population. Continuing professional development enables you to keep up with new developments in your specialist subject area and provides opportunities for you to refresh and develop your practice skills on an annual basis. Most professionals belong to organisations that have a formal system of CPD that is linked to their freedom to practise. The introduction of such a system for the learning and skills sector is designed to add value to your already comprehensive range of skills and increase your sense of professional identity through membership of the Institute for Learning.

What are the benefits for me?

You already have to work quite hard to keep up with your specialist subject. New research, evidence and analysis for almost every area of study appears on the internet frequently and often has an immediate impact on your teaching. You also need to keep up with changing policies, evolving initiatives, new teaching techniques and information technology. In a sense, you have an opportunity through a formal system of CPD to get some professional recognition for the work you do to maintain your skills and you will also have the benefit of membership of an organisation that supports you in managing your professional roles and responsibilities.

What are the benefits for my organisation?

Education and training organisations may have concerns about organising membership of the IfL for all their staff and providing sufficient opportunities for development. Having said that, they will almost certainly see a number of advantages to the formalisation of continuing professional development in the sector. The most important of these is probably that an employer can now know for sure that in any 12-month period, all their full-time teaching practitioners will have engaged in a number of development activities that have the potential to positively affect the quality of learner experience and outcome. What is more, those developments are logged and validated by a professional body that reflects the values and aims of the sector. In the long term, employers will be able to see the cumulative effect of year on year development and reflection.

Do I have to pay a subscription to be a member of the IfL?

There will be an annual fee. It is intended to be quite modest, but it is an essential element of most professional organisations. Just before going to press, the government stated its intention to pay the standard fee for each practitioner, though the situation may change in the future.

Does my CPD have to show obvious links to the new professional standards for teachers, tutors and trainers in the lifelong learning sector?

It is likely that any development activity you carry out will have some links to the standards, since they represent a broad mapping of skills and knowledge essential to good practice. Your employer may wish you to relate your developments to the standards for strategic purposes. However, the IfL say that the nature of your continuing professional development should be influenced by but not restricted to the standards. This is because the standards are the overarching professional ones designed to be demonstrated at threshold level in order to achieve the full QTLS. In that sense, CPD could and should go beyond those standards and levels of expectation as part of ongoing professional growth and reaction to change over time. Indeed, if you look at the IfL website at their suggested development activities, they include two extra categories not related to the professional standards for this reason.

I am so busy that CPD is not my priority right now. What can I do?

It helps to plan ahead. The CPD model will operate in a 12-month cycle. Some effective planning will mean that you can schedule in and prepare the way for some developmental activities you might like to do by yourself whilst taking account of training that will be provided by your organisation. If you put a note in your diary to review your CPD progress regularly, you can adjust your plans as necessary. Being busy is the nature of the profession, so the IfL will be unlikely to accept that as a reason for not doing what is required of you as a member. If you do feel so busy that you think you are unable to keep up with your own professional development then you could consider the possibility of a development activity that explores issues such as effective target-setting, time-management or even assertiveness. A further strategy could be to talk with your line manager about getting some time or support to fulfil your obligation to remain in good standing.

I cannot decide what to do. There are so many possibilities. Who can help me make the right decision?

You will probably find that there is always going to be more than one possibility worthy of your investigation. Making a decision so you can proceed with it is key to a successful outcome. You could discuss potential topics with your line manager or staff development personnel. Outlining some ideas with a mentor or trusted colleague may be an option. One strategy that would certainly be of use here would be to visit the IfL site when you have some free time to go through their development questionnaire. It has a number of statements relating to practice and for each one, you would have a choice of responses. For every response there will eventually be a number of possible development activities you could undertake together with some reflective tools. The important point is to combine doing something that interests and motivates you with something that will have a positive impact on your practice.

How will I know if what I am doing is up to the standard required by the IfL? I could spend time on an activity or project and then find it was below the standard needed.

This is probably less of a problem than you might think. The IfL have signalled strongly that they are very flexible about the exact nature of your CPD and they do not intend to be over-prescriptive about what it should be or how you should go about it. What they do want is some evidence that the activity has been carried out, that you were involved and that you have fully and honestly reflected on the outcomes and impacts using some reflective tools such as those provided in this book or on their website. There is the question of presentation and the usual standards of spelling, punctuation, style and referencing of course apply. If these skills are not your strong point, get your written work proof-read first. Better still address the issue as one of your development priorities.

I have carried out a development activity that I think could count toward my CPD. What do I do next?

Collect the evidence together and keep it safe. The next thing you will need to do is complete the reflection element. This part is particularly important because it is the part you will log directly with the IfL. To help you do this you could look at Chapter 2 and carry out some of the reflective activities suggested there in relation to your CPD. Alternatively, you could look at some of the reflective prompts attached to some of the activities either here in Chapters 4, 5 and 6 or on the IfL site. If you are already a member of the IfL, it will be a relatively straightforward matter to upload your activity details and reflections onto the site once they are completed. It is also worth checking at this stage how many hours of CPD you have left to complete for the cycle, so you can plan for further developments within the time as necessary.

I am not sure that I am really any good at reflection. I can rarely think of anything much to say. What can I do to develop my skills in this area?

It is important to address this because reflection is seen as an essential part of effective professional development. However, it is true to say that not everyone is naturally inclined to be reflective in the sense required here. You will find some useful points about reflection in the next chapter. In particular, you may find that the section on asking the right sort of questions will lead you to thinking in a more reflective way. You should be reassured that it is a skill that can be learned and looking at and doing some examples of the reflective exercises outlined there should help you deepen and broaden your skills. Another action you could take to develop reflection is to discuss aspects of development activities with colleagues or a mentor.

What would happen if I did less or more than 30-hours of CPD in any one year?

It would depend on the circumstances. If you are a full-time practitioner, then 30 hours is the minimum you can do to remain in good standing with the IfL and maintain your Licence to Practise. Part-time staff will almost certainly have a pro-rata rate to achieve and you would need to check with the IfL regarding your particular case. If there are circumstances such as illness causing long-term absence from work or you are unemployed for a period of time, you would need to let the IfL know of the situation as soon as you can because otherwise when you are ready to resume teaching you may have difficulties if your Licence to Practise has lapsed due to lack of development activity. If you want to do more than the 30 hours of development in any one year, that is fine. The IfL make it clear that the 30 hours referred to are a minimum requirement, not a restrictive quota.

Will I have a chance to see what other practitioners in the sector have done for their CPD?

Yes. Once you are a member you will have access to the members' site. There are plans to encourage and enable members to share good practice across the sector by posting their most interesting activity outcomes and findings there. This will also be a good networking tool for you and could provide opportunities for you to get involved in collaborative development activities, a real advantage if your subject area is highly specialised one.

Getting into the professional development mindset

For many practitioners, it may seem that you will have to develop lots of new skills and attributes just to get started with this more formal approach to your professional development. There is also quite a lot of new information to digest and new considerations to work into your busy schedules. For some of you that might feel like a daunting prospect. In reality, there are a few key strategies which, once adopted, would go a long way to providing you with a sound professional approach to any development activity you undertake. Interestingly, once you begin working on these skills and begin to incorporate them into your everyday practice, you will find the whole process of continuing development and reflection can increase your sense of professionalism, confidence and capability.

You could usefully work on developing the following skills.

- **Honest self-appraisal**. It is one thing to act as though you are confident as a route to becoming so for real. There is plenty of evidence to support such behaviour. However, it can be less helpful if you carry this attitude forward and convince yourself that you are beyond reproach in every area of your practice when perhaps you are not. Being completely honest about the things you are good at and the skills you need to work on is essential for effective self-development. It might therefore be very useful to you to organise some time to profile yourself in terms of skills, abilities and confidence as a prelude to seeking support for any sort of professional growth. Note your professional strengths as well those areas that you think could be improved. Those of you who like charts could carry out a personal SWOT analysis, outlining your strengths, weaknesses, opportunities and threats in relation to your practice. Those of you with a more right-brained slant to life could draw yourself a personal concept map with you at the centre and your professional life and ambitions radiating out from there.

- **Reflective observation**. There is a critical difference between observing an event and observing it reflectively. Observing something without the intention to reflect can be a bit like watching an interesting documentary. You may feel entertained and you may remember certain parts that resonated with your own attitudes but will the experience have changed you or your behaviour permanently as a result? Reflective observation calls for you to conduct some sort of dialogue with yourself about the nature of what you are observing and what can be learned from it in your own case. It asks you to look below the surface of the events you see. It encourages you to internally debate and draw out the possible alternatives and speculate on the impacts that such alternatives might have. Once you get used to activating this mindset, you could find it a crucial tool for critical evaluation, both of your own behaviour and the behaviour of others. There is further discussion about reflection and reflective behaviour in Chapter 2.

- **Professional curiosity**. When life is pressured, the best strategy to cope often seems to be to just to concentrate on getting through each day. If this is sometimes your reaction, you may need to actively engage your professional curiosity again. Children often go through a stage when their curiosity about life is apparent through the way they seemingly question everything. As we grow older, we tend to lose the skill of asking meaningful questions. You need to re-develop your professional curiosity. Question everything you can. Not just by saying the words 'who', 'what', 'where', 'when', 'why' or 'what then', but by asking yourself, and sometimes others, the sort of exploratory questions that can generate new thinking and ultimately new behaviour. One of the most powerful questions to ask yourself about your practice or your career is, 'What if?' What would happen if you did things a different way today? Develop curiosity about how colleagues acquire and use their skills and expertise. How do they know what they know? How do they do what they do? How do some of your colleagues manage to look as though they are so confident? Ask them. Listen, reflect and apply the feedback to your own practice. Once you know how they do it, you can do it too. You can read more about how to do this in Chapter 2.

- **Flexible thinking**. This is not the same as indiscriminate thinking. Flexible thinking is asking you to be objective and rule out bias from your internal dialogue. Set aside or challenge the assumptions you usually make. Be imaginative about possibilities. Look sideways for solutions to persistent problems. It also tends to put you in a more positive frame of mind when you think 'I can' or 'I will', rather than 'I can't' or 'I won't'. Flexible thinking comes from asking yourself the question, 'What other alternatives could there be here?' Being flexible can also develop from looking at problems or issues from different perspectives. How does this look from your learners' point of view? If you were mentoring someone else on how to manage this situation, what would be your best advice?

- **Flexible behaviour**. Having flexible behaviour carries many benefits for you and your organisation. It means having a whole range of constructive ways to respond to the many different and complex situations you encounter each day. It has the added benefit of reducing the stress that often comes with having to deal with unexpected events. Being adaptive this way allows you to change what you are doing when you perceive it is not effective. Changing your lesson plan mid-session and doing something different when you spot a strategy is not working is a hallmark of the confident and flexible practitioner.

- **Appreciation of context**. You do not operate in exclusion. You are part of a huge and complex network of teachers, trainers and tutors that drive the education, training and ongoing development of the entire post-compulsory sector. Without your input, industry would be less skilled, lives would be less fulfilled, opportunities for personal and professional growth in the work population would be curtailed. What you do in your classroom contributes to national wealth, economic development, international competition and personal growth for individuals. It is also worth noting that the way your institution organises itself and the very nature of your practice is shaped by government policy as a response to those factors. Appreciating the broader context of your role is part of being a true professional.

- **Theory awareness**. Not everyone has the enthusiasm or motivation to keep education theory uppermost in their mind whilst dealing with the practicalities of delivering education and training. Professional development however, does place some emphasis on your ability to make links, when you can, between what you do in the professional arena and the models and theories that may or may not underpin those actions. This does not mean that you cannot enter the classroom without a heavyweight volume of theory to hand but it does imply that you should develop the habit of directing at least part of your professional reflection in this direction. All of you who have achieved your teaching qualifications and those of you working towards them now, will have encountered a number of theories about teaching and learning. Many of you will also have come across theories and models related to reflective practice as part of the process. You have a part to play in the ongoing debate by examining those theories from time to time and questioning their pedigree and sustainability in the light of your own knowledge and experience. Theory is rarely static. It changes and grows through the agency of critical examination conducted by peers. Being reflective about the nature of education theory and how it works in practice can contribute to that process.

The code of professional values and practice

As you saw earlier in this chapter, one of the requirements for remaining in good standing and maintaining your Licence to Practise was that you should uphold the terms of the code of professional values and practice as set out by the Institute for Learning. This code is being developed by consulting across the sector with the aim of incorporating the vision, values and attitudes that the majority of practitioners subscribe to in the profession. It is due to appear on the website in full in 2008 and you would be wise to be aware of its main components when that occurs since you are meant to comply with them in order to remain in good standing. The IfL plan to publish on the site a set of statements that cover a range of shared professional values and the draft version for member consultation is on the website as this chapter is being written. The statements are intended to be aspirational; that is you should be aiming to incorporate them into your practice.

Further to this, there is to be a code of conduct that more specifically defines standards of behaviour expected of members in particular circumstances. Finally, there will also be a defined disciplinary process that would be used to investigate and take action in any case where the code had been breached. Currently it could be said to be an evolving document, though the draft section on shared professional values covers many of the areas and standards you would expect a document of this nature to include.

- **Respect for people**: This section would cover aspects related to learner safety and physical and emotional health, welfare, differing needs and equality and diversity.

- **Professional development**: Would aim to include reflective practice, skill and knowledge development, scholarly enquiry, collegiality and sharing of best practice.

- **Professional behaviour**: Would include relationship and behaviour management, effective communication with stakeholders, learners and peers, responsible behaviour including responsible behaviour with regard to the environment and the carrying out of duties with transparency, quality awareness and integrity.

- **Environment and community awareness**: Likely to focus on the conservation of resources, the minimising of pollution, raising awareness of environmental concerns, supporting social responsibility and respecting the multicultural nature of communities.

Whatever the eventual nature of the final documents, they will be worthy of your attention since they will define, in formal terms, the values and professional conduct expected of you as a practitioner. Furthermore, they will clarify procedures and processes designed to investigate allegations of unprofessional behaviour and breaches of conduct in order to protect the reputation of the Institution as your representative body in the sector.

A summary of the main Institute for Learning role to date

The Institute for Learning has been responsible for implementing the agenda set out by the government in *Equipping our Teachers for the Future*. In doing so it has:

- developed the framework for the conferral of Qualified Teacher Learning and Skills and Associate Teacher Learning and Skills (QTLS and ATLS);

- created the mechanism for the award and renewal of the Licence to Practise;

- set up the criteria to be met by every practitioner in order to remain in good standing;

- designed a positive and reflective model of continuing professional development linked to good standing and the Licence to Practise;

- devised and developed a code of values and practice that reinforces professional identity;

- organised the development of the technical architecture that will enable the registration and ongoing management of the system – this includes the creation of database, secure hosting, online tools for development and CPD portal.

Its ongoing role will be to manage and further develop the system for the benefit of all stakeholders, including you.

Summary of key issues covered in this chapter

- The underlying principles of the professional development model.
- The annual procedure for continuing professional development and requirements for remaining in good standing.
- Sampling procedures and quality assurance.
- Twelve frequently asked questions about CPD.
- Getting into the professional development mindset.
- The code of professional values.

2. Reflection and your professional development

Reflection in the context of your CPD

The philosophy underpinning the continuing professional development cycle is that any development in that context is likely to be more effective when conducted through the medium of reflective practice. The Institute for Learning is clear that you as the practitioner are central to that process. In that respect, reflection is not simply something that you should do to meet the criteria once a development activity has been completed; it is integral to the whole process of professional growth. It begins with you taking responsibility for examining your practice as a means to identifying your development needs. It continues with you setting out those needs clearly as a set of measurable objectives and engaging in activities to achieve them within a reflective framework. Those objectives and achievements, whilst they represent your particular development needs, also reflect your teaching context and the needs of your employer. The final element, the one that is lodged with the Institute for Learning, is the summative reflective one and it is that aspect we mainly address here. The whole process is shown in a simple form below and explained in more detail in the section after that. You will see that the part detailing the reflection element goes into more detail than the model of CPD in Chapter 1 does and this is to provide you with a range of reflection possibilities depending on the context.

The CPD process, emphasising the stages of reflection

● Reflect on your practice to date.
● Set out your development needs.
● Articulate them as measurable objectives.
● Carry out development activity.

- Reflect on why you selected this activity and what you have learned by doing it.
- Reflect on the impact the activity has had on your practice.
- Reflect on the extent to which the outcomes of the activity relate to the broader context in terms of sector priorities and developments.
- Reflect on the process undergone, possibly linking it to models and theories.
- Reflect on any further development needs highlighted in the process. These could feed into the next round of CPD if appropriate.

Let us look at these stages in some more detail.

Reflecting on your practice to date

There are a number of ways to do this, though they all require honesty and a willingness to be objective about your strengths and areas in need of development. Many practitioners argue that the best way to reflect properly on your practice to date is to spend time discussing it with someone you respect and trust. Even before you get to that point, you might find it useful to write down your thoughts about your professional life in some way. You could, for example, create a concept map that shows your practice as a whole. You may prefer to list your main professional skills and skills needs, or you may feel more comfortable with a SWOT-style personal analysis. Whichever process you employ, it helps to remember to include your successes and professional strong-points as well as articulating your perceived needs.

However, reflecting on your practice has several important functions. Not all of them are so closely related to identifying the more obvious development opportunities. It is also the case that reflective practice can promote a deeper evaluation of the meaning behind what you do and the way that you do it. Furthermore, it can promote a clearer appreciation of the social, economic and political context in which you conduct your practice. Examining your usual assumptions or everyday behaviours by looking at them in a new way will probably also suggest some interesting avenues to explore for your development, particularly if you feel able to challenge the conscious and unconscious processes that influence the way you think and act.

Setting out your development needs

Before you begin to draw out your development needs from the above process, reflect for a moment on the differences between 'needs' and 'wants'. Development 'needs' indicate a possible skill or knowledge deficit, either now or in a future role. 'Wants', in this context, may be driven by personal interests, preferences and ambitions not necessarily linked to your current role or the requirements of your employer. Both are probably important to you though it is wise to maintain a sensible balance between improving your current practice and growing your career in the broader sense. Some of your development needs might be critical to your work role and possibly should be given priority. Other goals may be important but less urgent. It would be fine to highlight all of your objectives even if some of them are longer-term ones and not likely to be achieved within a single CPD cycle.

Articulating them as measurable objectives

When you have clear objectives in your lesson planning, your teaching tends to be more successful. You know what it is you want your learners to achieve by the end of the session and that clarity enables you to devise better teaching strategies and clearer methods of assessment. Similarly, when you can clearly state what you want from a professional development process and set your objectives out in an unambiguous manner, you can then also be clear about what you need to do to meet your outcomes. This means when setting your development needs down you should aim to use 'clean' language, the sort you probably use when you set objectives or learning outcomes for your learners. Many practitioners set objectives for learners by prefacing them with the phrase 'by the end of the session, the learner will be able to...' This approach leads naturally to words that describe the desired behaviours. It would not be out of place then, for you to articulate your development needs in a similar way: 'By the end of my CPD activity, I will be able to...'

If you would like to look at setting objectives and learning outcomes in more detail, it is covered in Chapter 5, as one of the development activities you could opt for.

Carrying out the activity

There is quite a lot written elsewhere in this book about the nature of the development activities themselves. Here though it is important to emphasise that reflection is not just something carried out once the activity is completed but an important element of the process as a whole. This means that you should aim to reflect during the development process as well as at the beginning and the end. You could ask yourself questions such as, 'What am I learning here?' 'Is it what I anticipated?' 'If some aspect of this feels uncomfortable for me, why is that?' 'What sort of learner am I?' 'What else needs to be done?'

Reflecting on why you selected the activity and what you learned by doing it

Sometimes you will find that a development activity has been chosen for you. Your employer may have strategic aims that require you to master specific knowledge and skills. If that is the case, it is fine to say so in your reflection, though if properly done, you would want to include how you felt about being directed in this way. In many cases though, you will need to devise a number of development activities for yourself. When this happens, you have the opportunity to investigate something that really interests you. It may not be helpful though to say, 'I chose this activity because I thought it would be interesting', since that statement does not indicate much in the way of reflective thinking. If, on the other hand you said, 'I chose this activity because I have always been curious about the links between theories of learning and ways I could test them out in the classroom', then reflection is evident in that activity selection. The most usual reason for choosing a particular development tends to be that it is likely to have a positive impact on your practice in some way. Perhaps it would help you to improve the learning experience for your learners. If so, say why you think that would be the case. Perhaps you feel it would increase your confidence and sense of professionalism. To be more reflective, go into more detail about why you feel you need to improve in these aspects. Generally though, whatever the undertaking, it should aim to increase your practice-based knowledge and skills and alongside that, develop your confidence and competence as a practitioner. You can also address what you have learned by doing it, not by offering a list of outcomes achieved but by reflecting briefly on how you intend to integrate this new learning into your professional behaviour and how aspects of your practice might develop as a result. That way, you have offered some real reflection on the experience as opposed to simply reporting what you did.

Reflecting on the impact the activity has had on your practice

This is an interesting thing to do because it is asking you to observe yourself and your relationship with your learners and colleagues objectively and take a 'before and after' approach to the analysis. What effect has the development had on the way you carry out your role? What impact has it had on your learners and colleagues and how do you know? You may wish to ask them for some feedback or perhaps you will see the impact in the quality of learners' work or the quality of their behaviour. If you are ever unfortunate enough to participate in a development activity that you feel has contributed little or nothing to your professional knowledge and skills, your reflection would still be important. This is because if you are able to say why you feel the activity was ineffective, you are half-way to carrying out some useful reflective analysis. If you then go on to discuss how, in your view, the activity could have been managed more successfully, you will have demonstrated that you have learned something useful, particularly if you can offer some relevant theory to support your thinking. In the previous reflective category, it was suggested that you could discuss what you had learned by doing it by referring to your practice. Here, you could look back after a period of time and properly evaluate the longer-term impact the development has had.

Reflecting on the broader context

You and your institution do not operate in isolation from the world outside. Indeed your role is likely to be one that enables others to take their place in it and play a meaningful part in the global economy. The economic climate of the twenty-first century means that workers need to be competitive, flexible and ready to learn new skills throughout their working lives. To an extent this philosophy is reflected in almost every learning institution in the sector in the way that syllabi and related assessment processes are devised and managed.

So you could usefully reflect on the extent to which the principles of the global economy and all that goes with it affect the nature of what and how you teach. An example of this could be the way that certain types of courses have developed in recent years, whilst others have all but disappeared or, why certain age groups and occupational areas tend to enjoy greater funding support than others.

At a more local level, you could observe the way broader aspects of local economic and social policy impact directly on your role and from a different direction, the impact and influences aspects of your practice might have on the community.

Reflecting on the process of development

You could argue that every event offers potentially the opportunity to learn something if you can reflect on it well enough. Looking carefully at your own learning processes when undergoing any sort of development can help you to identify and embed the more useful elements. There is also a considerable amount of theory about the nature of learning and development processes that you could use to add some academic underpinning to your reflection. For example, what principles of learning were applied in the way the activity was managed? Did they work for you? If yes or no to that question, why should that be the case? What does that signify about the way you learn?

Reflecting on your further development needs

It is best to think of your continuing professional development as just that: a continuous, cyclical process that grows with you over the course of your professional career. Every development you undertake has the potential to reveal new insights into the complex world of post-compulsory education, where new knowledge and the skills required to put that knowledge into practice seem to change daily. It is likely then, that when you go through some new learning experience in the form of CPD, the process will reveal some further development opportunities that you may not have considered up to that point. It is helpful to keep a note of these potential new development needs to discuss with your line manager next time you meet to review your performance. Certainly if you can justify development activities in terms of increasing your skills base and potentially producing more effective results for your learners, you may find that you have the support of the people who are in a position to fund you.

Finally, it is worth adding here that not every development activity will necessarily lend itself to reflection in every category outlined above. It is also worth saying, however, that most development activities could be discussed reflectively using the above headings and the Institute for Learning encourage you to do so whenever you can.

Why reflection is more than just thinking

Imagine that you have just finished the final learning session in a very busy teaching day. You had prepared your lesson plan and created some additional resources to facilitate a more effective level of learning. You had done everything you felt you were supposed to do, but the session did not go as well as you anticipated. Not everyone seemed to grasp the points you were trying to make, some learners looked bored, others seemed dispirited. Clearly, not all the learning outcomes were met by everyone and as the session drew to a close you felt a bit less sure of your skills as a teacher.

Thinking about the above scenario might lead to these statements.

- I wish I knew what I had done wrong there, it all seemed to fall apart as the lesson went along.
- I cannot believe that so many of the group failed to grasp what I was trying to teach them. Perhaps it's because half-term is coming and everyone is tired.
- I feel as though I am not as good a teacher as I previously thought, perhaps I am not cut out for this job.

Thinking is a useful activity of course but as shown here it often fails to identify the real problems and tends to lead to an unhelpful mindset because of the haphazard nature of many thinking processes. What would probably be more useful would be if you could replace 'thinking about' with 'reflecting upon'. Reflection, when done well, avoids blame and speculation and looks for solutions, leaving you feeling more in control. It is also more likely to ensure that you will learn from the process and be better able to deal with any similar situation in the future.

Reflecting on the scenario above might include the following observations.

- If I had been observing that particular session instead of teaching it, what would I have felt needed to be done to make more effective?
- What are the most common reasons, from a theory point of view, why learners might fail to achieve the objectives set for learning session? Could one or more of those factors apply in this case? If they do, I could come up with one or two strategies to overcome them.
- My instant reaction was to feel like a bad teacher but I know how to do it properly and blame doesn't help me to put things right. I will go back to my plan and devise some new and better strategies for differentiated learning to ensure the next session runs more successfully. Then I can review my new approach again later.

The difference between thinking and reflection is that here at least, the thinking has led to a negative and unhelpful frame of mind that fails to improve the situation for anyone, while the reflection avoids blame and leads to a more objective and solution-focused outcome with a clear plan of action.

Which approach would you rather take and which looks most like the one a true professional would take?

Thinking, reflection and mental models

Another essential part of being reflective is to recognise that we all cannot help but bring certain deep-rooted assumptions and ways of seeing the world to the way we think and act. This is because we construct mental models from our individual life experiences, and yours are unique because your life and your experience and interpretation of it are unique to you. As we grow, our mental models act as a filter, helping us to interpret events and manage our lives without becoming overwhelmed. In a sense our mental maps are like Donald Schön's 'theories-in-use'; we use them to make decisions and generate actions based on what we know and what has happened to us in the past. When we apply our mental models to events around us and the process seems to bring results, our thinking can become more like entrenched beliefs and from that point we tend not to challenge them; unless of course we sometimes subject our beliefs and taken-for-granted assumptions to a process of reflective examination. This is important, since mental models, because they affect the way we think, also strongly influence our behaviour. Furthermore, even if the mental models we have adopted are negative or unhelpful we still tend to interpret most of our experiences through that particular filter. For most of us this means that whilst we might have little dispute with first-order information – facts that are provable – when it comes to interpreting the meaning or implications behind them we are back to working through our own personally constructed mental filter. That may be why there tend to be so many conflicting yet often equally plausible theories to explain almost any event. The data are rarely disputed once they are established as fact but the explanations, the why or the how, are dependent on the way each theorist uses their unique mental map. So, what does all this mean for you as a reflective practitioner? In essence, it means that you need to be aware that mental models, your personal mental maps, encourage you to think in certain ways, often without examining if there could be an alternative approach or explanation. Simply by remembering this, you are more likely to approach reflecting on your practice in a more constructive way.

For example:

- You could ask yourself some searching questions about any situation, such as 'Why is this so important to me?'
- Challenge any underlying assumptions you might have about a situation that are not supported by evidence. Who says this is the case and why? What would happen if things were done differently?
- Take a different view from the one you normally adopt and know that you are doing it. Be curious about different perspectives and how the same event can be interpreted in different ways. Ask, 'What would happen if I did things a different way?'

- Seek out alternative explanations from the one you arrive the most easily at. What other reasons are likely or possible?
- Attempt to see certain events through different eyes. How does this probably look to the learner, a professional observer, your line manager, a supportive colleague? Are their perspectives any less or more valid than your own? Why might that be the case?

Such self-questioning indicates that you are moving towards adopting and using reflective strategies as a route to more deeply engaging with your professional world.

The difference between 'doing reflection' and being reflective

Professional reflection is potentially a key development tool for any practitioner in the sector. The question needs to be asked though about just how effective the process really is when it is done without the spirit of true reflection being present. 'Doing' reflection has become an almost compulsory component of practice, linked as it often is to such processes as formative and summative evaluation of teaching and learning. There can even be assumptions made that evaluation and reflection are the same in everything but name. However, the level of introspection encouraged by some self-evaluation models has the potential to produce damaging levels of self-criticism and this can be particularly the case when the process lacks a solution-focused direction. Similarly, the level of reflection, particularly of the single-loop kind seen in some self-assessment questionnaires, can lead the less experienced practitioner to an unhelpful level of 'tick-box' complacency. In both the cases here, the reflection and the processes linked to them, it could be argued, have become ends in themselves, which is not what true reflective practice is about. For reflective practice to have any real impact where it matters, the reflection has to move beyond examining professional behaviour in the intellectual sense, no matter how well done that is, and become translated into practical outcomes. Without that stage, the opportunity for transformational change is missed and the reflection remains as internal dialogue with nowhere to go.

Of course, even when reflection does lead to changes in your practice, there would be a need for you to reflect on those developments carefully later, and possibly make further adjustments before you could assess their true value. When you are a reflective practitioner, as opposed to just going through the motions, it becomes part of your professional persona, as opposed to something you do because you are compelled to complete a process for quality assurance purposes. You won't have to say 'I had better do some reflection now' because once you have developed the skill, it will become integral to your professional behaviour. You won't be able to help doing it. Many people say that applying some of the principles of reflection to their life outside of work has a positive effect in their non-professional world too. In other words, perhaps reflection should be a way of life, not just a way of work.

Developing the skills of reflection

Many of you will probably already be quite comfortable with the concept of reflective practice and applying reflective thinking to aspects of your everyday practice. Some of you may feel less certain about exactly what it is that you are supposed to do, particularly in order to do it well. Some people suggest that reflection is pretty much the same as thinking and thinking is certainly one of the skills you need to reflect, but it is not the only one, as you will have seen above. It helps if you think about the purpose of doing it. Why reflect on your practice at all? Generally it is to help you to be even better than you already are at what you do and challenge your limiting styles of thinking and behaviour as part of that process.

Steps to competence

When you are developing your skills of reflection, you move through similar stages to anyone undergoing a new learning experience.

- You begin with a state of *unconscious incompetence.* This sounds a bit like an insult, but it simply means that at this point, you don't know what you don't know. You are not aware that you need to learn something or even that the potential exists to learn it. You may however have the issue brought to your attention, which brings the process to the next stage. So in the case of reflective practice, it has come to your attention that it exists and that you are being asked to show evidence that you can apply reflection to your professional role.

- At this stage, you move to a position of *conscious incompetence.* You now realise that there is a possible gap in your knowledge or ability and once the nature of this gap is explored, you can go about obtaining information and training to move yourself forward into a position of competence. The stage of conscious incompetence is one that often generates the motivation to learn. In the case of reflective practice, it is here that you might actively seek out learning and support from a mentor or start reading and thinking about how to go about developing the skills you need.

- After a period of learning, you may find that you are able to do things in a way that you couldn't do before but you still have to think carefully about what you are doing at each point. This stage is known as *conscious competence*, though as you continue to practise, you will probably find that you are able to act more competently without mentally talking yourself through each bit of the process each time. At this point, you will begin to feel that you are becoming a reflective practitioner without having to mentally rehearse processes or models and it will start to feel a more natural process.

- *Unconscious competence* is the point when you can do something skilfully without having to consider each aspect before you do it. In terms of reflective practice skills, you might feel here that reflection has become so natural to you that you don't have to think about it. Whilst feeling this way in some learning situations could be useful, you also need to actively maintain reflective awareness by bringing reflection into your conscious thinking when the situation calls for it. So, you may act in what feels like an instinctive way when an unplanned situation arises, and your unconscious competence at this stage helps you to manage the unexpected. Later however, it would be wise to also consciously examine the event, using your reflective knowledge and abilities in order to learn from the experience.

REFLECTIVE TASK

- Re-examine the steps to competence set out above and relate them to a learning experience you have been through as an adult.

- Explore your own experience of learning and moving through each stage. Express it either through writing it down, drawing a representation of the experience, or discussing it with peers.

- Which stage was the most challenging one for you? Why was that?

- If you are unconsciously competent in that skill now, why might it still be important to apply reflective thinking to it from time to time?

- In terms of reflection, which level of competency best describes you?

- How might your learners benefit from you carrying out this exercise?

Models and theories that can support your reflection

The following models and theories about reflection and the reflective process could be employed to examine aspects of your practice as part of CPD. They have differing levels of complexity but the thing they all have in common is that they have evolved from observation and reflection on practice over time. Some of them are relatively unstructured and less prescriptive, whilst others are more structured and have clearly defined processes you would need to work through. If you know what kind of learner you tend to be, you will probably feel drawn to some approaches and not others. That is fine. There is a lot to be said for taking an approach that you feel comfortable with. However, it could also be the case that you would develop new perspectives and alternative insights from occasionally working with models that are less familiar to you. The models and theories shown below are just a few of the processes and tools for reflection that practitioners have found to be effective. There are many more. Investigating some of the less well-known ones could be a potential CPD activity in itself.

Flanagan: Critical incident analysis

This approach from Flanagan (1954) suggests that in order to understand the world from the perspective of another person, we must strive to put ourselves in their position and see the world as they might do. For example, if you were trying to see the world from the perspective of one of your learners in order to understand their behaviour better, you would need to take yourself back to a time when you were learning something new and unknown, just as they are now. You might have felt excited, vulnerable, anxious or shy in such a situation, possibly a confusing mixture of emotions.

Applying critical incident analysis then, would mean posing some searching questions, and attempting to answer them from the point of view of that other person. You could try questions such as:

- What emotions did I feel in that situation?
- How did I want or need others to behave?
- What did their actual behaviour signal to me?
- What were my main worries and concerns about that situation?
- What might have been the best course of action to take to protect or help myself?

If you could reflect sufficiently from the point of view of the other person, using your own memories of being a learner to help you, Flanagan suggested that you were more likely to be able to empathise with the learner's perspective and thus be able to take action to support them.

Flanagan also suggested that if you are able to reflect clearly about your own past experiences (in this case, a former learning one), you are better able to develop your own skills of reflection, analysis and empathy and use them to improve your practice, for the benefit of all your learners. Interestingly, it could be argued that naming this approach 'critical incident analysis' suggests that it is only appropriate when something particularly troubling or unpleasant has occurred. This is not really the case because Flanagan meant it to be used to examine all aspects of practice, ranging from the positive to the negative. So a critical incident could be when something went particularly well, as well as when something went less well. A second issue sometimes raised is that as a model, it is rather vague about the process of examining the critical incident itself. There is no prescriptive set of actions or procedures to follow and some teachers are more comfortable with a clearer, more structured framework.

Use it:

- if you are comfortable examining the perceptions and feelings of others or would like to develop greater empathy with your learners;
- if you are able to recall your own life experiences and can harness those feelings to connect with other people in a similar situation;
- if you are curious about how feelings can affect behaviour;
- if you see a lack of structure as permission to explore and reflect;
- if you would like to develop the skill of critical incident analysis.

Explore alternatives:

- if you are not comfortable or confident in assuming how other people might be feeling;
- if you find it difficult or stressful to equate your own learning experiences with the experiences of others;
- if you need step-by-step guidance to manage the process.

It is worth saying that if you feel uncomfortable with any model of reflection, for whatever reason, you can usually find another that will feel right for you. However, there is also an argument for suggesting that you consider discussing your discomfort with a mentor, coach or trusted colleague rather than attempting to avoid it. You could then consider using such a discussion to frame a self-development activity for your CPD.

The DATA process

The DATA process (Peters, 1994) is a simple but effective model that is so startlingly logical that it is curious that no one had thought of it before. It is intended to be an instrument for examining practice issues and solving practice problems by moving through the following process.

- **Describe** the issue or practice problem.
- **Analyse** what has been described in order to uncover any assumptions that are being made about the incident or the choices available to solve it.
- **Theorise** potential solutions.
- **Act** on the best potential solution to emerge from the process.

The main advantage of this model is that using it enables you to step away from the immediate emotion of the issue and deal with it in a more objective manner. This process is further enhanced if you are able to work through it with a trusted colleague or mentor, who can act as your 'critical friend' and challenge gently any underlying assumptions about the case that you might have missed if you had been working through it alone.

One drawback with this model has been said to be the lack of an evaluation element following the 'Act' phase. Rather than discounting the model altogether, you could quite easily adapt it by including some reflective evaluation at the end of the process that critically examines not just the outcomes of the 'Act' phase, but re-evaluates your thinking on the assumptions and theories that were part of the process.

Use it:

- to examine practice issues or problems that would benefit from some emotional distance;
- if there are likely to be underlying assumptions about the situation that would be useful for you to tackle;

- if the situation is not immediate or requiring urgent action;
- if you prefer a structure to follow.

Explore alternatives:

- when the situation requires prompt or immediate action;
- if you have yet to find someone you trust to support you as a critical friend;
- if you find that the structure of this model is too prescriptive for the way you prefer to think about problems.

Brookfield's critical lenses

Most of the models we tend to use as education practitioners are designed to support the examination and reflection of specific events. Brookfield (1995) offers a model of reflection that invites you to focus on the same event from a variety of perspectives. These 'critical lenses' suggest that any practice event requiring reflection should be viewed in the following manner.

- **From your own perspective**. What happened as you experienced it, how you felt and how you behaved. This detail is probably better if recorded in some way, particularly if you intend to work on it over a period of time.
- **As viewed by your colleagues**. When you talk over an event with a colleague, particularly when a situation has had a strong impact on you, it is likely that they could offer a different interpretation of the event from the one you have formed. This may be because it is easier to be objective when one is not directly physically or emotionally involved. Discussing a key event with one or more colleagues could help to moderate any tendency you might have towards over-interpretation and it also reinforces the notion that your own interpretation of the event may not be necessarily correct or shared by everyone. Even if you are unable to discuss your situation directly, it can help to imagine how a colleague would respond to the incident and what interpretation they would be likely to place on the event.
- **From the perspective of your learners**. Some objectivity can be gained from gathering feedback from learners. It is also possible that they have experienced the event in different ways and drawn conclusions about it that you have not considered. Even if you do not ask them directly, but instead, put yourself in their position regarding the event, you are more likely to appreciate their point of view.
- **From the perspective of theoretical literature**. Brookfield's fourth lens through which to examine and understand an event is that of existing theory. This is an important element since theory can help to explain why events occur and what we as practitioners can do to manage them more effectively. It also reminds us that theory evolves from practice and practice develops from theory on a more or less continuous basis and that we are part of that process.

Use it:

- to get more of an objective perspective on practice issues;
- when you are curious about how theory can support you to solve practice problems;
- when you can call on learners and colleagues to provide you with perspective.

Explore alternatives:

- if you need to act quickly;
- if you are not comfortable empathising with the feelings of learners or colleagues.

Using the work of Schön as an aid to reflection

Donald Schön developed many of his theories about the nature of reflective practice from the observation that there was a fairly obvious incongruence or mismatch between what he called 'means and ends' in education. In short he was highlighting the development of an outcomes-based approach to education that seemed less concerned with the process of learning than the product. Schön described this situation as a separation between 'knowing and doing'. In other words, we as practitioners 'know' the theory relating to good practice but may, for a variety of reasons, adopt ways of doing things that are less effective because they are expedient. He was raising the issue of the potential gap between what he called the 'technical-rational' knowledge we learn as theory in our own training and the reality of real-life practice, where theory can often appear inadequate to deal with our day to day problems in the learning environment.

He also argues that practitioners tend to have practical knowledge about their role based upon what he calls 'knowing in action', which arises from the experience of doing what we do every day. You might prefer to call it instinct or intuition and skilled teachers use it all the time. It is part of having the unconscious competence that comes from experience, though Schön calls them 'theories in use' since they tend to be taken for granted and are rarely examined in any meaningful way. A key element, then, of being an experienced and capable practitioner according to Schön would be to stop and examine our 'theories in use' every so often because they may require revision as we, our learners and the state of knowledge changes over time.

Schön also developed the concepts of reflection *in* action and reflection *on* action to describe the reflective processes that occur during and after a learning session. Reflection in action was likely to happen during the course of a learning session. Perhaps you would spot that your learners seemed confused or perhaps you would see that everyone had achieved the objectives more quickly than anticipated. Reflection in action would be an immediate response to the feedback you were getting and would likely result in an on-the-spot adjustment to your lesson plan to accommodate this new situation.

Such behaviour depends upon a degree of flexibility and confidence that tends to emerge with experience. It is true however, that less experienced teachers might find the call to reflect in action and potentially change their approach mid-stream a cause for anxiety, since it would mean moving away from the structure of their lesson plan.

It is worth considering then, that reflection on action could be the key to effective reflection in action. Imagine that you had just finished teaching a session and you were aware that during that time, most of your learners appeared to have failed to grasp the main point you were trying to make. If you were unable to reflect in action, you probably ploughed on hopefully with the plan because you were not confident enough to act laterally to achieve the objective. So far, not so good. However, if you were able to at least engage with the process of reflection on action, afterwards, there is potential to learn from the situation and develop your reflective confidence at the same time. Reflection on action is a key part of the reflective process from Schön's perspective because it takes place soon after the session but is sufficiently removed from it to allow you to reflect on your actions objectively. If as part of that process you are able to think critically about your actions and reflect on how you might behave if a similar event was to occur again, then reflection on action may lead to a more confident reflection in action next time you are faced with another practice dilemma.

If you would like to examine aspects of your own practice using some of Schön's theories, here is a brief summary of the concepts discussed.

- The separation between knowing and doing: happens when you know the theory about good practice but find yourself acting otherwise, perhaps because it is easier or will save time.
- Knowing in action emerges from your experiences over time. You may feel that your professional behaviour and decisions are more like instinct or intuition supplemented with confidence when you feel this way. You can often spot it if you are observing an experienced practitioner at work.
- Theories in use are your taken-for-granted assumptions about what you do and the way that you do it. Theories in use tend to grow out of knowing in action and becoming professionally confident, but Schön suggests that you need to identify and re-examine your theories in use from time to time, since assumptions that once were sound in one context may no longer be valid.
- Reflection in action is enabled through the development of theories in use. You find that with experience and reflection your behaviour becomes more flexible and responsive in the learning environment because experience has taught you that acting in the present can benefit your learners now.
- Reflection on action is a process of examining recent learning events with the aim of learning from them so as to be able to improve your practice and deepen your professional insights and understanding. Reflection on action can also be harnessed to improve reflection in action in future learning situations.

Single-, double- and triple-loop reflection

When you are working on developing your skills of reflection in relation to your practice, there are a number of approaches you can take to enhance the process. One of them is to note the difference between single-, double- and triple-loop reflection and how they can be applied to your practice experiences.

Single-loop reflection

Single-loop reflection identifies that there is an issue to note or problem you need to deal with. When reflecting this way you can usually describe the event in detail, what went well and what went less well for example, and devise actions to take to eliminate those factors. However, in single-loop reflection the learning from it is limited to that particular issue, so when the original problem recedes, so does the learning that came from it.

Some questions you could ask that fall into the single-loop category are shown below.

- What went wrong there?
- Why did 'X' happen?
- What could I change that would stop it happening again?
- What worked well there?
- What could I do to ensure I can do that again?

Double-loop reflection

Double-loop reflection involves the diagnosis and solution stage identified above but has an extra loop in the process that prompts you to not just learn from that event but to reflect on how such learning could be applied in similar cases in the future. It is this abstraction, this moving of events away from the concrete and into generative thinking, that is the real difference here. Generative thinking allows you to stand back from the incident, examine some of your assumptions, view the events in an objective way and theorise potential solutions as though it were an objective case study. This approach could enable you to solve a practice problem but it will also enable you to develop your own 'theories in use' as identified by Schön (1987). Theories in use can inform, with the aid of reflection, your practice behaviour in the future should the same or a similar situation occur. Thinking this way can also help you to avoid the 'must try harder doing the same' response to negative events and replace it with the 'reflect, learn and try something different' approach. It would seem, then, that double-loop reflection is more experiential and developmental than the single-loop model.

Some questions you could ask that fall into the double-loop category are shown below.

- When a teaching and learning session goes well, how do I know? How do I judge the evidence? What do I compare it to?
- When a teaching and learning session goes less well than expected, how do I know? How do I judge the evidence? What do I compare it to?
- If I plan to do something different next time, on what basis do I choose what to change? What evidence, derived from implicit or explicit knowledge, supports my new choices?
- What assumptions do I make about my learners? How might those assumptions affect my behaviour and the assessment decisions I make?

Triple-loop reflection

Triple-loop reflection will perform all the stages described above in the double-loop process and then examine and further challenge the thinking behind them. It does this by going both inside the process and by standing outside it to understand it better. To go inside the process you need to question your own motives, beliefs and underlying behaviour in relation to your professional world. To examine your practice from outside the process, you may want to consider it in the wider social, economic and political context to identify the influences those systems may have on aspects of your role. Beyond that there are even further issues to consider that centre on beliefs, values, the nature of power and the nature of knowledge itself. Triple-loop reflection can examine any or all of these areas in the search for the underlying nature of your practice.

Some questions you could ask that fall into the triple-loop category are shown below.

- How does what I teach and how I teach it reflect current government policy and economic principles? If I am aware of those principles, should my learners also learn how their working world is shaped by them?
- How comfortable am I about the shifting definitions of education and training and their relationship with economic policy?
- Why is some knowledge considered more important or valuable than other types of knowledge or skill in our society?
- Are my personal values ever compromised by my work role and, if so, how should I behave?
- What motivates me to teach others? What do I get from it beyond a salary each month? What is my philosophy of practice and are there any assumptions behind it?
- Are there any hidden agendas in the syllabi I teach, perhaps more by what is excluded rather than what is in there? What assumptions underlie what learners learn?
- What are the underlying values of the system of examination and testing? Who benefits most and least from this process?

Asking yourself further reflective questions and using prompts to generate reflective thinking

Despite the fact that reflection as a concept is widespread, it is possibly a taken-for-granted assumption that everyone knows how to do it. Even so, it is not unusual to hear people say that they find reflection a bit of a challenge, particularly beyond the double-loop stage. Part of the problem could be the gap between theory and practice, where you can be properly versed in theoretical models of reflection but still feel unclear about how to apply them in relation to your own practice concerns. In the context of your professional development, however, there are a number of questions you could ask yourself and prompts you could employ to generate the sort of reflective responses you might be searching for. Try some of the questions below to promote some deeper reflective thinking after a development activity. The prompts that follow after that are designed to promote reflective thinking too, though they come at the task from a different direction. Answering a number of these could also form the basis of a post-activity return to the Institute for Learning.

Some questions to spark reflection on development activities

- Why did I choose to do this activity and not a different one?
- What have I learned about myself during the process of doing this activity and reflection?
- What impact, actual and potential, has this CPD activity had on me, my colleagues and my learners?
- What links could be made between this development activity and wider sector policies and concerns?
- Has this process identified any further skills I want or need to develop?
- What steps do I need to take to turn the reflections on my development activity into positive outcomes for me and my learners?
- If I were to do the same development activity again, what would I consider doing differently and why?
- Were there any unexpected outcomes for me from doing the activity and reflecting on it afterwards?
- Did I have any 'taken for granted' assumptions about this development activity? What were they? How can they be challenged?
- How might the impact of my CPD extend beyond my immediate learners and into the world beyond?

Prompts to generate further reflection

Rather than answer a question as you might do with the above, to complete these, you develop a response by expanding on the unfinished statement.

- One published theory I can identify as related to this development activity is...

- One theory of my own I have developed about this matter is...
- When I come across lots of different and competing theories to explain an education issue it makes me feel...
- This CPD activity has helped me to understand...
- My top three strategies for implementing what I have learned are...
- One aspect that still puzzles me is...
- I could share the most important aspects of this development activity and outcomes with colleagues by...
- Another skill or aspect of knowledge I now wish to develop is...
- One assumption of mine that has been challenged by this process is...
- The most useful model of reflection to me at this time is...
- My role as an educator reflects government priorities because I...
- Education and training has outcomes that extend beyond work for my learners in that...

Using feedback as a tool for reflection and self-evaluation

Many people assume that feedback is by its nature designed to emphasise the negative. As teachers we tend to accept that positive feedback to our learners is more effective in permanently changing behaviour and improving performance. This approach also applies to you and your practice. Get into the habit of asking yourself what went well in your teaching and why, as well as what was less effective. When you ask yourself, 'how did I do that?', you are gathering feedback that shows that you are prepared to pay attention to what works as well as to what doesn't.

Feedback on your performance can come from internal or external sources. External feedback can be gathered from your learners or other professionals in a position to occasionally observe you. In the case of your learners, ask them how they think the learning went. Was there anything else they needed in order to reach their learning objectives? How do they prefer to learn? Such feedback will help you to calibrate your teaching and learning strategies to their changing needs. External feedback may also come from an observer sitting in on a session. Your tutor, your mentor, your line manager, a peer or trusted colleague may be able to offer you a different perspective on your teaching from the one you tend to get from your learners. It is especially useful to seek verbal as well as written feedback from such an event; it will give you the chance to ask questions and clarify any points you are less clear about. Internal feedback is equally as important, some would say more so. How did you feel about a particular situation? If you could go back and re-live that situation, what would you like to do differently this time? Learn to pay attention to this reflective inner dialogue and if you are worried that you will forget it all, write it down or record your thoughts in some way. Giving yourself feedback is not just about evaluating the extent to which you and your learners achieved the objectives set, or the quality of the resources you supplied, important as those factors are, it is also about asking how and why and what if in relation to events.

The real skill here when reflecting on your practice is giving attention to detail because it is often the small things that have the most impact. What makes the difference, for example, between you going into your class and conducting it with confidence and feeling nervous and exposed? When you know the answer to that, you have uncovered the difference that makes the difference for you and you can act on it to become more confident in the future.

Using reflection as a tool for modelling key behaviours

This sounds more complex than it really is. Modelling is a form of imitative learning. Bandura (1977), a prominent cognitive psychologist, suggests that one of the main ways we learn is through observing and then imitating other people. This is done, he says, by careful observation of the role model, followed by the imitation of the role model's behaviour in a certain situation using visual memory as support. You can probably see how this behaviour could be useful to you if you were expanding your professional skills by observing and imitating or modelling the desired behaviours. It is also helpful to appreciate this theory in the context of the way your learners may imitate you and your behaviour as part of their development. Bandura's theory is outlined below, though it is discussed here in the context of your professional development rather than in the context of education in general.

Social learning theory of imitation

To learn successfully by imitation Bandura says you need to do the following.

- **Pay attention**: You have to decide to observe to learn in this way. The amount and the quality of the attention you give to this process depends upon the extent to which you like and/or admire the model you are observing. The learning is also affected by your expectations of the event and what it can do for you. From a reflection perspective, this means that if you decide to observe someone because they have particular skills that you wish to acquire and you approach it systematically and reflect on what you have seen afterwards, you have set yourself up to learn. So you might go to observe someone with some clear ideas about what it is you are hoping to capture during the session. You might think: 'I would like to concentrate on how Jackie uses her resources to keep the group busy and learning and I also want to see how she manages to deal with any unwanted behaviour'.

- **Remember what you have seen**: When you have observed your role model, you will need to identify which aspects of the model's behaviour you wish to emulate particularly and remember it in such a way so that you will be able to recall it when you need to. You may have a mental picture of the event at first, though later you will probably recall only the elements that were the most important for you. This means that if you really want to learn this way, you will need to rehearse the observed behaviour mentally and imitate this behaviour physically, if you wish to retain it. From a reflection point of view this means you need to be clear in your own mind about which aspects of behaviour you wish to adopt and why.

- **Model the behaviour**: When you first imitate your role model, you may feel that you lack some of the essential skills to do it well or that you are acting in some way (conscious incompetence, to borrow another term). Over time though, Bandura argues, most people learn and develop their skills by copying their desired actions until they get them right and they become second nature (unconscious competence). This means that observing a role model does not guarantee that you will absorb and reproduce those skills at once, though following a period of reflective modelling, thinking about what went well and what didn't and why, you may achieve the result you are looking for.

- **Be motivated**: Bandura suggests that harnessing different types of motivation can support learning this way. External reinforcement, perhaps in the form of encouragement from a mentor, could convince you that this is a useful learning process to undergo. Alternatively, you may feel motivated by vicarious reinforcement. This where an observer sees that the model is rewarded in some way for their behaviour and you wish to be rewarded in a similar fashion. Many of you will also be motivated via self-reinforcement, believing in yourself and your ability to successfully develop new behaviours. From a reflection standpoint, this means gathering information about yourself and what drives you to develop. Once you understand which sorts of motivation work for you, you will be able to ensure you seek it out to support you in your search for professional growth.

As a learning process, it is one that you already know how to do. As a child, you learned most of your early skills, particularly those such as speaking and relating to others, by imitating family members, and many people would say that copying or imitation or modelling is a key part of learning anything new from riding a bike to becoming a successful teacher.

The neurolinguistic approach to modelling desired behaviour

Some approaches to this type of learning go further than Bandura's theory by suggesting that modelling should be more than imitation and motivation. Neurolinguistic programming argues that the most effective learning takes place when the learner not only imitates the obvious behaviour of their desired model, but goes further still. In this approach, the most effective outcomes emerge from not only from imitating the teaching behaviour you wish to master, but also by adopting aspects of the model's underlying physiology such as their body language, voice, tone, pace of speech and even their breathing pattern. This means that you should practise standing how they stand, breathe how they breathe, adopt similar voice and speech patterns and develop similar gestures and responses. Then, the theory suggests, you will get the sort of outcomes they get with their learners. The neurolinguistic 'extras' can make all the difference when they supplement Bandura's imitation and motivation.

Based on the thinking above, here are seven steps to effective modelling of behaviour that anyone could try.

1 **Select** someone who has the sort of professional behaviour you would like to adopt as your own.

2 **Decide** which aspects of the person's behaviour you would like to emulate. Perhaps you want to be as relaxed as they seem to be or maybe you want to feel more in control of learner dynamics. Whatever the behaviours are that you wish to capture, be clear about them.

3 **Observe** the model carrying out their role. Sometimes unexpected events give you the opportunity to reflect on your assumptions. For example, you may believe that a particular person is so good at what they do that they never have any problems. What you see is more likely to show you, if you reflect, that they have as many challenges in a typical lesson as anyone else. What probably will be different is the manner in which they respond to and deal with any difficulties. Look out for what makes the difference and reflect on how you can usefully incorporate such behaviour into your own teaching.

4 **Identify** specific aspects of the model's behaviour that you could emulate. How do they establish and maintain rapport with their learners? How do they present themselves at different stages of the session? How do they use their voice to manage, persuade, reward, set tasks and keep control while remaining approachable? Do their clothes and the way they wear them give them an advantage? How do they sequence delivery of the learning in a way that works for every learner? What part do their resources play? How good is their timing? You can model each aspect if you identify each component and examine it carefully.

5 **Discuss** professional practice ideas with the person you wish to model. Ask questions about aspects that still puzzle you. Ask them how they developed their skills and what they still do to maintain them. This advice can also be modelled by incorporating the most useful bits into your own practice routines.

6 **Model** the desired behaviours in your own teaching and learning environment. Introduce them a bit at a time and note and reflect on the effect they have on you and your learners.

7 **Model** your own successful behaviours. When you adopt strategies that work, you can use reflection to help you identify exactly what you did and how you did it. You may even be able to link it to theory. When you know what works and you know that reflection gives you the context, you can apply that learning and experience even in new and less familiar situations.

Keeping a reflective journal

A reflective journal can be an excellent tool for practitioner development. There are a few things you need to have in mind when using one if you want it to be effective.

- **Write regularly**. Not necessarily every day, though. It is not a diary but a journal. When you look back, you will see how your ideas develop over time.

- **Be objective**. This means you can use your journal to discuss particular aspects of your practice that are challenging you in some way without laying blame or making value judgements.

- **Be honest**. The chances are that you will be the only one who reads it, so be completely frank about your concerns and feelings. Once you are clear what they are, you are in a better position to deal with them by searching for a solution.

- **Look for solutions**. Consult colleagues and note down their responses. Identify and examine useful theories. Use all these ideas, together with your own reflection, to decide on the best strategies to adopt.

- **Challenge your own thinking**. Ask yourself questions. Is there another way? What assumptions am I making that could be questioned? Is this my opinion rather than fact? Is this what really happened or is it how I feel about what happened? How would another objective person see this event? If this had happened to a colleague, what would I advise them to do?

- **Treat the process as a positive journey**. If you expect to find a solution, then you probably will, eventually. Remember, if you want something to be different, you need to act. Reflection can give you the tools to think through a problem but it is action based on reflection that is most likely to bring results.

Writing your journal

Getting the best from a reflective journal depends on what you put into it in terms of quality and effort. For the free thinkers among you, the good news is that there are no real rules about how it should be done, just advice and suggestions like those shown here that you can follow if you wish. For those of you who like or need more structure to your endeavours, the process outlined below might help you to get started when tackling specific problematic practice issues. It may take some time to arrive at a solution you feel is right, so be patient.

- **What is the event or situation?** What happened to prompt this journal entry? Outline the event, giving the facts only at this stage.

- **How did I feel about it at the time?** What were my reactions? Were they helpful?

- **How do I feel about it now?** Away from the situation, do I feel any different? Why should that be the case? What can I learn from that reflection?

- **What is an objective view of the event?** How might this look to another observer or a supportive colleague? What would my mentor be likely to say? What would I say if I observed this happening to someone else?

- **How can I learn from this?** Are there any theories or models to support my developing ideas and potential solutions? What opportunities are there for constructive changes to be made?
- **Can I identify two or three actions I could take to prevent a similar situation in the future?** Note them down; keep them simple at this point.
- **What do I need to do to get the process going?** Identify your aims and desired outcomes in more detail here.
- **What support or help do I need to do this?** Do I need more information? Is there someone I trust who can support me while I do this? What other resources do I need? How can I get them?
- **What was the outcome or impact of my new actions?** Evaluate the response to your different behaviour. Do I need to make any further adjustments?
- **What have I learned about myself and the issue by going through this process?** How could it help me now and in the future?

REFLECTIVE TASK

Keep a regular reflective practice diary for at least six weeks. At the end of the period, assess the value of the process in terms of the contribution it has made to your ability to manage the conflicts and demands of professional life.

Summary of key issues covered in this chapter

- Addressing the reflective aspects required by the Institute for Learning.
- Why reflection is more than thinking.
- The difference between doing reflection and being reflective.
- Models and theories that can support your reflections.
- Engaging with single-, double- and triple-loop reflection.
- Using questions and prompts to generate reflection.
- Imitation and modelling of key behaviours.
- Writing a meaningful reflective journal.

3. Maximising your CPD potential

CHAPTER OBJECTIVES

This chapter is designed to:

- explore training opportunities and strategies that will enable you to get the best from your professional development;

- suggest how you can maximise opportunities for capturing evidence of development;

- identify the key strategies and approaches you will need to address to complete a return to the Institute for Learning.

The LLUK standards and the new culture of professional development

When you look at Chapters 4, 5 and 6, you will see that the activities there are linked to Domains A–F of the New Professional Standards for teachers, tutors and trainers in the Lifelong Learning Sector (www.lluk.org). Lifelong Learning UK describe these domains as 'the overarching professional standards for full QTLS status [Qualified Teacher Learning and Skills]' (LLUK, 2006). In essence, they are the threshold standards that practitioners in the sector need to achieve in order to gain their teaching qualification and their licence to practise.

Having established that, the CPD activities, tasks and reflective exercises set out in this book are intended to take you beyond those standards by encouraging you to explore and develop aspects of your knowledge and practice in a personal and professional reflective context. This does not mean that the tasks and activities are necessarily 'harder' or more complicated than the ones you encountered when working towards your QTLS. In many ways, the opportunities for engaging in continuing professional development are potentially much more satisfying because the developments you undertake in this context are more likely to reflect your particular practice interests and priorities. Even if institutional targets and strategic aims and objectives influence aspects of your professional development (and they are bound to at times), there is in place now a culture of expectation, and even entitlement, to continuing professional development over the life of your career.

Balancing your training needs with institutional objectives

There is every chance that at certain times in your career, your line manager may require you to undertake some development in an area that does not feel like a priority for you. This is not really surprising since your manager may have different targets to meet as part of a strategic plan. You have a minimum of 30 hours professional development to undertake in each 12-month period if you are a full-time member of staff, with pro-rata arrangements for part-timers. Thirty hours is generous if you enjoy professional development and potentially onerous if you do not, so below are some ways to maximise your CPD potential.

- **Cultivate your curiosity**. Be alert to emerging development opportunities that match your changing responsibilities and interests. Talk to development staff and mentors about what you would like to do, and see what they suggest. Ask your colleagues where and how they learnt to do what they do. Check out appropriate professional websites for training and conference dates.

- **Be flexible**. One of the best ways to get the most out of training is to be open-minded about a whole range of potential training opportunities. Yes, you may be very keen to do a certain short course but if someone else controls the funding and has different priorities, what can you do? In most cases it is wisest to embrace whatever training is offered. Chances are that it will be useful and pragmatically, you will be able to count it toward your IfL annual tariff. There is always another year. Remember too that 30 hours of CPD per annum is the minimum training that professional standards require, so you could always do more if circumstances allowed.

- **Negotiate**. There are a number of opportunities each academic year for you to put your case for a particular development activity you would like to undertake. Many practitioners have regular meetings with line managers and you could put your request on the agenda. Appraisal and/or performance review also provide you with the means to make your particular development needs known. Furthermore, in such formal circumstances your training needs will almost certainly be written into a document that is retained and reviewed later. This is a key time to set some training objectives, so go into any meeting of this type armed with information and sensible strategies to achieve your goals.

- **Mix modes of development**. Over any 12-month period your professional development activities could include attending a conference, taking part in an in-house training day, carrying out a self-directed activity such as those outlined in Chapters 4, 5 and 6, or completing a short course. Teachers know that for most learners, variety promotes learning and teachers are learners too. Mixing modes of professional development can be stimulating, energising and sometimes even inspiring. It can put your practice into perspective and if some of it is carried out in groups with colleagues you don't usually work with, it can potentially provide you with a whole new network of support.

What counts as professional development from the IfL perspective?

The Institute for Learning are keen to be as inclusive as possible on the question of which development activities qualify to be acceptable evidence. This means that they are flexible about the nature of any development you may undertake as long as you retain evidence of it and complete the reflective element and log it with the IfL. They also accept that the 30 hours per year that each full-time practitioner should complete will most likely be the result of a number of differing development activities undertaken during that period. That said, it is clear that they also expect that the evidence of participation, learning, evaluation and reflection for each element should not only be robust and verifiable but also remain available for scrutiny as part of IfL quality assurance and quality control measures. We have already established that full-time practitioners will have to provide evidence of a minimum number of hours of professional development per year. It is likely that for most people their 30 hours will be the outcome of a different range of activities each year and that the nature of the developments undertaken will alter as professional priorities change.

Below are some examples of professional development that could be used as evidence for the IfL. There will be other real-life situations that are not included here. If you are in any doubt about the nature of your activities and want to be sure that they qualify, you can contact the IfL (www.ifl.ac.uk) and they will be happy to help you.

Sources of professional development

Continuing professional development comes in many guises. For the purposes of this section, they are divided into three areas: in-house training, external training and self-directed development. Within each of those areas there are a host of possibilities and they are discussed here in terms of their potential strengths and drawbacks for you as a participator or institutional provider. The discussions around in-house and externally supplied training include some simple models for reflection that you could use to harness such an experience in a manner that would be acceptable to the IfL. (The reflective tools for self-directed development appear in Chapters 4, 5 and 6 alongside the activities and you will also find some alternative reflective material in Chapter 2.)

In-house training

This area subdivides into two sections. The first deals with training provided by in-house staff who are usually well known to the participator. The second section covers training provided in-house but delivered by an outside body especially commissioned for that purpose. In both cases, opportunities exist for you as a practitioner to record the experience as part of your annual tariff of CPD with the IfL. Evidence would need to be available of your attendance and participation at any event, together with your personal written reflection composed once you had evaluated fully the impact of the event, more details of which appear later in this chapter. There is a raft of factors that both support or detract from each mode of development and these are outlined first. They may be helpful when you need to decide which types of development to engage with.

In-house training delivered by in-house staff

This is probably one of the most frequent forms of staff-development activity carried out in institutions. It has a number of benefits.

- **Proximity**. All the staff involved in the process, including the trainers, are usually in the vicinity, if not on the same campus. This reduces development travelling time and costs.
- **Availability**. In-house activities can be matched to the ability of the staff to attend. In some cases normal timetables can be suspended for the duration of the training or the same training can be offered at a number of points to maximise access.
- **Immediacy**. The training can be generated for the specific needs of the institution at any particular point in the academic calendar.
- **Economy**. Specialist and externally delivered training can be costly. In-house development can make use of expertise that exists within the institution.

On the other hand, there can be a number of difficulties inherent in this approach to staff-development.

- **Specialist availability**. Some smaller institutions might struggle to find specialists in certain professional areas.
- **Professional objectivity**. When training involves developing new or different approaches to practice, there is, many would argue, a need for an element of professional distance that can best be supplied by someone from outside the institution.
- **General validity**. Many in-house training days cater for large numbers of staff in one session. Given that staff are likely to be diverse in knowledge, experience and even motivation, there can be a question mark over the extent to which this sort of training can be much more than an information transfer process unless it includes active participatory elements that embed individually desired outcomes. Furthermore, any validity only tends to be verifiable, in this respect, at a later date when training is translated into practice (if indeed that is the outcome). Currently, a great deal of training relies on a brief end-of-session evaluation from participants as its only evidence that the process has been worthwhile.
- **Specific validity**. If in-house-training is to have the potential to provide meaningful evidence of development for individual practitioners, it will have to include the following: It would need to be linked to one or more of the professional standards for CPD as set out on the IfL site. It would need

to provide verifiable evidence of the development details in the form of a programme of events and activities. Finally, it would need to generate from every participant an individual reflective response that met the standards of reflection required by the IfL. This would suggest that any in-house development would need to consider these aspects carefully at the time of setting up the training so they could provide staff with the evidence that a specific training session would count against their personal tariff for CPD.

In-house training using outside developers

Bringing in expertise from elsewhere in the life-long learning sector to deliver training in-house is another approach. It has many, though perhaps not all, of the benefits of proximity, availability and immediacy described above. Economy however may be affected by consultancy fees or at the very least, the travel expenses of the speaker.

Further advantages are often said to be:

- **New light through old windows**. Experts from elsewhere in the sector can bring a new or different perspective to training. It can be energising and refreshing to look at familiar topics in a different way. Many people would argue that the reframing of objectives that often accompanies a new trainer can lead to innovative thinking and fresh approaches to tackling old issues.
- **Choice**. There tends to be a wider pool of experts to draw from in the sector as a whole than exists in most institutions.
- **Assumption neutrality**. There is no 'hidden history' or labelling based on previous interactions between trainer and participators to get in the way of potential development. Learning can therefore take place in a value-neutral setting that enables individuals to be different people for the duration, if they so choose.
- **Role-changing**. Participating practitioners have the opportunity to be learners again without affecting existing staff dynamics in the institution.

Having said that, there may be concerns about the following.

- **Cost**. External trainers can be expensive even when they prove to be good value for the money.
- **Risk**. Training briefs and marketing pitches can look impressive but unless one has used an organisation before, the quality of the training will be unknown until the training is in progress. Furthermore, the training could be of the highest quality but still not match the desired learning outcomes of the institution well enough.
- **Value and validity**. Some people doubt the value of this type of training in terms of outcomes. Staff may have a good time and go away enthused but unless it can be demonstrated that real and lasting positive changes occur in practice as a result of it, how do we know how effective it really was? This means that long-term evaluations may be needed to justify the financial outlay.

- **Staff availability**. It may prove difficult to get all the potential trainees together at the same time. If there are too many absentees on the day it reduces the unit value of the exercise and raises the unit cost.

External training and development

The main factor that underlines most of the activities in this category is that the venue for training tends to be set away from your workplace. Participators usually have to travel, sometimes quite long distances and the training is likely to be lead by people unknown to you. Distance learning, either by correspondence and CD-ROM or more likely via the internet, is an exception. In this case, the training is remotely supplied but the venue for training may well be at your personal computer in your own office. Some of you may be able to carry out all or part of this type of learning from home if you have the right software.

This sort of training covers a very wide range of potential development possibilities and can include:

- attending a conference/forum that is connected to your subject specialism;
- attending a conference/forum that is focused on aspects of curriculum and/or sector policy;
- participating in a one-day or short training course relevant to your subject specialism;
- participating in a one-day or short training course relevant to aspects of curriculum and/or sector policy;
- participating in a longer-term part-time course relevant to your subject specialism or curriculum issues;
- work experience in the industrial or commercial sector linked to your subject specialism;
- undertaking a distance learning course relevant to your subject specialism or curriculum area via the internet or similar means;
- engaging with remote one-to-one coaching from a specialist coach or mentor via telephone and email;
- face-to-face one-to-one coaching from a specialist coach or mentor.

Main advantages of this type of training are listed below.

- **New perspectives**. They provide a refreshing alternative to in-house training; different surroundings, new faces and a change to normal workday routine can aid motivation and increase active participation.
- **Networking**. The chance to meet, engage and form professional links with staff from other institutions. Many people see this opportunity as a key benefit of attending external training. Even internet courses tend to have trainee forums where you can forge useful working relationships with other learners.

- **Role-switching**. Candidates may have the opportunity to play a different role from their usual professional one while in training. This can be stimulating and promote the sort of creative, lateral thinking and problem-solving strategies that there usually is little time for in the standard busy work schedule. Being a learner again can also remind you how it feels to be in that position and can therefore be an aid to certain reflection processes.

- **Support and recognition**. Staff who have been supported with money and/or time to attend courses or conferences are more likely to feel valued by their institution than those who do not.

- **Value-added learning**. The learning generated and the information gleaned can be 'cascaded' to the home institution on return without too many additional costs.

- **Valuable resources**. External training often provides high-quality, re-usable resources for participators.

- **Personal attention**. In the case of one-to-one specialist coaching and mentoring, the training can be highly specific to individual's development needs.

That being said, there may be some problems.

- **Differentiation**. External group training, particularly for large numbers, is rarely devised with participators' specific learning needs in mind. This means they may not cater for individual differences to the extent seen in a college setting, for example.

- **Social barriers**. Some people might find the unfamiliar surroundings and training methods inhibiting rather than stimulating. This can be overcome on a longer course but on very short courses it can remain a bar to active participation for shyer members unless effective ice-breaking strategies are employed at the outset.

- **Cost**. It can be expensive. There is often a fee for attendance, plus travel to and from the venue. Some activities may necessitate a hotel stay. It will also be likely to generate costs for staff cover.

- **Speed of delivery**. The fleeting nature of many types of short training courses may mean that developments that could be potentially useful are not given sufficient opportunity to embed themselves in memory and behaviour and thus are lost through lack of application and reinforcement.

Maximising the learning and reflection potential of in-house and externally led training

For most practitioners, the chances are that each year a proportion of your development hours will be generated through attending either in-house devised activities or training organised and supplied through outside providers. In both cases you will need to do a number of things in order to ensure that any development can count towards your annual tariff as set by the IfL and they are shown below.

- **Get the evidence**. When you attend the development activity make sure you obtain written evidence of the event that includes the date, hours involved and the programme of learning that took place. You will also need evidence that you attended the event. You should retain copies of this paperwork for possible IfL verification and quality-assurance purposes.

- **Carry out the training with reflection in mind**. Whilst you are taking part, note down points that will help you to reflect in a professional way. You may find handouts and a copy of the programme will help you to write up your thoughts later.

- **Complete the reflection**. It may be better if you reflect at two stages after a development activity. The first could be straight away when you could ponder on the value, as you see it, of the exercise in terms of learning both for you and the potential impact for your learners. For example, you may have learned something new and your learners may benefit from the way you integrate that new learning into the curriculum. The second stage really needs to be some time later, when you can review the extent to which any development has provided long-term benefit to you and your practice. If you intend to do both stages, it might be wise to put this in your diary for about four to six weeks beyond the original activity and reflection.

- **Store the evidence safely**. Those of you with access to a PC may wish to log with the IfL each piece of development reflection as you do it up to the 30 hours each year. Once you have registered with the Institute, that should be a fairly simple process. Others may prefer to gather together more than the minimum hours of evidence first and select the best examples of reflection to post to the site or send in the conventional mail at the end of that process. Either way, it would be important to keep copies of each piece of reflection you send to the IfL together with all the development activity details that you retain at work. This is because any aspect of your development in this respect could be subject to potential sampling by the Institute to ensure that professional standards are being maintained across the sector. If your name is selected, you may be asked to provide the IfL with all the paperwork and other supporting evidence that the activity was carried out and reflected upon in a satisfactory manner. Alternatively an IfL-appointed person may visit you at your workplace and review it there.

Reflecting on in-house, externally led and self-directed training experiences

If you are about to attend or have recently been present at some form of training or carried out a self-directed activity, you may wish to include it in a return to the IfL as evidence of professional development. As you will see above, you need to gather some evidence of the event and your active participation in it. For most people that part is straightforward. When it comes to the reflection part, however, there can be a tendency to do a version of the following:

- provide a detailed description of what happened at the event or during the development process;

- carefully evaluate the training and the trainer or your own performance when carrying out the process.

Whilst both of the above are capturing aspects of the experience, they will not necessarily be considered reflection in the professional sense. Most reflective models encourage you to look at any incident or situation from different perspectives in order to develop or maintain professional objectivity. Furthermore, viewing events in this manner can also provide contextual understanding. This means that any reflection you write up should aim to deconstruct your development using an approach similar to the one set out under the headings below. Ideally, each area shown here should be addressed whenever you complete a reflection, although it is likely that the emphasis you place and the amount you write will shift between the five areas depending on the nature of the experience.

- **Personal perspective**: Why you selected this particular development activity as opposed to any other that you might have done. What drew you to it? Was it a challenge to your current way of thinking or doing things? What have you learned about yourself in taking part?

- **Professional perspective (1)**: The extent to which the activity and what you learned from it has or will have impact on your practice. This part is considered particularly important, so it is very useful here to give one or two clear examples of the actual differences you expect it to make to you as a professional and to your learners or colleagues.

- **Professional perspective (2)**: The extent to which the outcomes of the activity link and relate to the broader life-long learning context in terms of sector policies and priorities. You may be able to link your development activity to funding priorities, a particular initiative or the strategic aims devised by your institution. Those of you interested in such issues could go further back still and explore the political, social and economic context in which your development has taken place. Another approach in this area could be to explore the potential benefits and impact of sharing your learning outcomes with colleagues.

- **Theoretical perspective**: Are there any theories or models that you can relate to this development activity? You would not be expected to go into major detail about theories but explore ideas related to them, particularly how they may link to the development activity in question. This could include using a reflective model to explore an event. You would, of course, be expected to reference your sources correctly.

- **Reflecting about reflecting**: Again, the IfL consider this element to be particularly important. You can discuss briefly the process you have undergone whilst carrying out this activity and reflection. How has this experience affected you? To what extent has the experience changed your behaviour, thinking or approach to your professional role? Did theories and models assist you, or did you create or adapt one? What are the three most important aspects learned and why are they important to you? There are a number of other routes to reflection that you may find useful in Chapter 2 and some further reflective tools you could utilise in the final three chapters that deal with self-directed activities.

Self-directed development by individual practitioners

Many practitioners will find that at least a part of their annual professional development will come under this heading. At first glance it may be daunting to have to identify, investigate, analyse, report and reflect on an area that may be unfamiliar. However, it could also be argued that that is exactly the point of professional development. It should be, at least in part, generated by your own interests and needs rather than those driven by institutional strategic objectives.

Plus points for this approach to professional development include:

- **Autonomy**. You select and manage this element of your professional development.
- **Flexibility**. It can take place at any time.
- **Choice**. You can chose something that motivates you.

Whilst that all sounds very positive for those of you buzzing with ideas and in possession of sound time-management skills, it may raise some anxieties for others.

- **Decision-making**. Settling on one topic can be an issue. A good starting point here would be to go to the activities in Chapter 4 that ask you to think about your current skills and professional interests. These may then direct you to certain development activities that might suit you. Another strategy would be to go to the IfL website, www.ifl.ac.uk, and start exploring the section on self-analysis. You could also discuss your ideas with a mentor, line manager or colleagues. The important part here is to explore and discuss but make a decision that feels right for you. Whatever you settle on will need to motivate and stretch you professionally in order for it to be effective.
- **Getting started**. If procrastination was a key skill, most of us would be comfortably qualified! Beginning a new project can be hard for some. Others rush in, work madly for a bit and then lose impetus. Get a file started. Put times in your schedule each week to review your progress. Set yourself at least one small task towards it each time.
- **Keeping going**. Remaining focused is the key to success with self-directed development. It is easy to lose direction, particularly if you are not certain where you are going with a project. Ask someone to act unofficially as your coach/mentor and meet with them regularly. Even 15 minutes every two weeks would give you a point at which you could report/discuss your progress or concerns. Perhaps you could do the same for them in return. If either getting started or keeping going are your major worry, be sure to read the part below that looks at harnessing your motivation.
- **Managing time**. Teachers tend to be fairly skilled at managing time since they tend to have lots of experience of lesson-planning and learning delivery. Nevertheless, professional development in this context could extend over a 12-month period, perhaps longer. Furthermore, this process

will be forever competing with countless other professional duties and obligations. It may be useful to have a long-term time plan for any such activity. Select an end date, a time when you estimate that the task will be completed and the reflection composed, and work backward from there. Allow some breaks and put in mentor time if you are fortunate enough to have one. Make sure this plan is integrated into your work schedule, so you can review it regularly.

Motivation management in self-directed development

It seems particularly important to manage your motivation when working on a development activity of this nature, not least because there are some obvious links between motivation and effective task management. However, motivation is an odd thing: left to its own devices it will often revert to 'idle-mode'.

Your brain needs to know what you want specifically in order to get you to your desired outcome. There are some tactics you can employ to switch it on and understanding something about how your motivation operates will help you select the best path to success. There are different types of motivation you can harness. If you have ever lost sight of your goals in the past, knowing what they are, how they work and how to tweak them to your advantage could be useful.

The key here could be to understand your motivation direction. Most of us seem to have developed concept maps that indicate a preferred motivation direction. We either tend to move towards the things we want in life, or we tend to move away from the things we don't want. In practice, both modes can be helpful, but away-from and towards motivation work in different ways.

Away-from motivation is mainly about the avoidance of discomfort, either physiological or psychological. It is very useful in removing you from danger but it is less useful when employed in a professional context. The trouble with this type of behaviour is that once you have taken steps to move away from a problem, skirted round it or avoided it in some way, you start to relax and your drive fades. However, in most cases the problem itself does not disappear and you can expend quite a lot of energy in displacement activities that help you avoid dealing with it when you are motivated this way. Furthermore, if you are concentrating on what you don't want, you are much less focused on what you do want, so you are likely to suffer from goal-drift. If that were not enough, because this away-from behaviour is about not wanting something, or avoiding something, it tends to put you in a negative state of mind. It is a common enough situation. You find yourself thinking something like: 'I am never going to finish all this marking. I am going to have to give up my whole weekend to do it.' Thinking like this doesn't really get results. If it did, you would have tackled the issue before it got so pressing.

You will have a much greater chance of success if you deliberately re-state your intention in a more positive way such as: 'It will be great when by Saturday afternoon I have done all my marking. Then I can relax and enjoy the evening.' So adopting toward-motivating tactics, where you identify a positive outcome for yourself, could be the solution to harnessing your motivation when managing your own development too. The following simple steps may help you in defining and moving towards your professional development goals. Furthermore, you may find them useful when you are searching for strategies to motivate your learners.

- **Be explicit** about what you want to achieve. Clarity and focus are important here, so be specific about what you want. Write it down as you see it and add plenty of detail. Read it out aloud to yourself. If you are a particularly visual sort of person try to imagine yourself carrying out this new behaviour and achieving your goal. If you are the sort of person who goes by 'gut-feeling' imagine how reaching your goal will make you feel.

- **Set a realistic time** for you to reach your goal. Too far away in time could demotivate you since there would be little sense of urgency. Too short a time might seem too pressurising and induce paralysis. Set a date that feels right for completion of your goal now and put it in your diary.

- **Borrow a few simple techniques** from seasoned motivators. Devise a path from where you are now, to where you want to be with this development. Some people see this route as a flowchart. The more artistic among you could map it out on paper. If you do, make it as detailed as possible. Put in some short- and medium-term goals along the way. If you are a list maker rather than an artist, use larger and more colourful print than usual to itemise your goals. Once you have produced your plan, put it where you see it regularly. If you are someone for whom words are key motivators, you could talk yourself through your plan or set aside a few minutes now and then to discuss your progress with someone you trust.

- **Take one step**, no matter how small, each day toward your development goal. It may just be a phone call or a search of a website. Just do something. The results you want will come out of actions, even small ones, as long as they are taking you in the right direction.

- **Put a note in your diary** to review your progress frequently. Take few minutes to reflect on what you have done since the last review to move you closer to your goal. Anticipate your next action and how you are going to go about it. Some people find that it helps to record their reviews in some way. Noting down how you are feeling and what you are thinking at each stage could be very helpful when you come to write the reflective part for the IfL. If you work and think best when you interact with others, ask a mentor or trusted colleague to be your sounding board and talk it through with them.

- **Continually imagine the end result**. Think clearly about how achieving your goal will feel and how you will become more professional as a result of this process.

- **Adopt a positive attitude**. Not only is it a nicer mental state to be in, it can affect the outcome of your efforts. If you start out thinking 'I've done this sort of thing before and it didn't work for me' then it probably won't work for you now. Rephrase your outlook with something like, 'I will achieve my development goal because I am clear and focused about what I want to do.'

People who adopt this approach often report that once you start to actively focus on specific goals, something interesting seems to happen. You begin to notice coincidences. Articles appear in journals, programmes pop up on television, or you may meet someone who has special knowledge or just the sort of information you are looking for. This is synchronicity at work. Your brain, because it now knows clearly what you want, is operating behind the scenes, scanning for information. It will be sifting incoming data and focusing you on things you might have ignored before you became so clear and specific about your goals. Finally, because you have made your development goals clear and framed them in a way that means something to you, you will be able to move clearly towards achieving them.

Using the web to support your development activities

Most of you will be confident in your internet search skills though being able to evaluate and even critique information you find on sites, rather than take it at face value, is a skill that you may need to demonstrate in the reflective element you lodge with the IfL. When you carry out development activities and subsequently complete your reflective evaluation, you may find yourself searching the internet for theories or examples of practice to underpin your findings. Below are some points to bear in mind during this process.

- **Truth and objectivity are difficult to verify**. Remember that search engines exist for mainly commercial reasons and therefore are not entirely value-free. The sites they show up in their results, especially the top 100 or so, are not necessarily the best ones in the objective sense. The sites shown tend to be in the top ratings because they have ensured that their web page bears as many key search words as possible. It helps then, to be as specific as you can in the selection of your keywords when you initiate any search.

- **Do some detective work**. Use the web addresses of sites as a clue to their origin. This will tell you something about the extent to which you can trust the content. The extensions often give the game away; for example, in the UK any URL ending with .ac.uk is likely to be an educational establishment. One ending with .gov will hail from a government or government-sponsored site. A bit of caution is advised for sites ending with .co.uk, .org or .com since anyone can own one of those for a price, though it has to be emphasised that for the most part such sites are genuine and reputable. Having said that, commercially owned sites tend to supply sound information but probably lack impartiality. If you spot a ~ in the address or %, this implies that this is almost certainly a personal site rather than one generated by an organisation. Once again this does not mean you cannot trust the information found there but you would be wise to double-check the details with another source to be sure. There are some useful sites that will check the origin and by implication, the credibility of web pages for you. Try www.archives.org.

- **Store web addresses**. Note down good and useful sites as you come across them and keep that information somewhere readily retrievable. Regular researchers often have their own web address books full of their best finds. If you intend to quote from one, or cite information from pages located on the net, be certain to note sources accurately to avoid accusations of plagiarism. Using links to related sites can be helpful, though make sure you don't get so sidetracked that you forget the purpose of your original search.

- **Exercise healthy cynicism**. Don't believe everything you read, no matter how convincing it looks. Employ your critical judgement with all information. Guard against opinion dressed up as fact. Even sites that claim to be value-neutral or value-free rarely are and others may have a commercial or political bias. This does not necessarily render their offerings useless, rather it signals that there are probably other perspectives on the subject in question that are not covered there. Some sites have almost legendary followings; Wikipedia for example is often cited by learners as though it is an authoritative source, yet many of the entries there tend to lack the accuracy, objectivity and provenance that are desirable for truly academic and professional work. As a theory source then, you might want to exercise caution but welcome it as useful background.

Language, style and referencing

Since the main written element presented to the IfL will be the reflective part of any development you have undertaken, it is useful for you to remember that reflection is a tool for you to analyse your experience and relate it to aspects of your practice. Therefore, it would be quite acceptable for you to use the word 'I' where appropriate. Many of you will know from experience that objective writing that excludes the first person tends to be the holy grail of academic prose. However, when you are reflecting on an experience that has happened to you, writing from a personal perspective is very difficult to avoid. The following strategies for maintaining an acceptable standard of language and style may be useful.

- Use 'I' when no other word feels right, but avoid beginning every sentence that way. 'I' overused tends to imply that you are only seeing the world from you own point of view and are not demonstrating an appreciation of perspective.

- One of the other cautions about using the first person is the tendency to follow 'I' with opinions rather than verifiable facts. Check your reflective writing for opinions and ensure they can be supported by evidence or theory. Opinions are often built on assumptions and assumptions need challenging as part of the reflective process.

- Remember that reflective writing can, and often should, include looking at events from points of view and perspectives other than your own.

- Avoid 'slang', jargon and colloquial language. Aim for a sensible, reasoned style.

- Proof-read your work for spelling and grammar. If you put it aside and read the finished draft again after about a week, you will usually be able to spot glaring errors. Inconsistencies will also tend to show up then; if you said in paragraph one that you were going to address four points and only came up with three, this is when you will probably notice what you have done.
- Check that what you say is what you meant to convey. Is there a better way to express it now that you are looking at it again?
- Acknowledge the work of others in informing your reflection by referencing carefully.

Referencing and plagiarism

It is likely that you will use some substantive material at some point when writing your reflections. Check the IfL website for their preferences about referencing. If you are unable to do that, you can safely assume that the Harvard system of referencing will be acceptable. Some of the main points are set out below, though if you are a referencing novice, you should seek out some support from a mentor.

- The main purpose of referencing in this context is to ensure that ideas, models and theories developed by others are properly acknowledged in your writing. This is necessary to avoid accusations of plagiarism, which means intentionally or unintentionally passing off someone else's work or ideas as your own. You may wish to reference material at any point in the CPD process; perhaps by consulting books and other sources to inform your development activities or the reflections that follow them.
- Keep referencing simple and consistent. It matters less which model of referencing you use than that it should be used by you in a consistent manner. So if you begin by using the Harvard format, it is best to keep to that throughout.
- If using direct quotes in your written text, you will need to include the author's name, the date the work was published and the page on which the quote can be found. For example, 'The tendency to believe that a particular theory is true directs our behaviour attitudes, to the exclusion of other competing theories.' (Hillier, 2002, p.14)
- If you were to simply refer to Hillier's point here without quoting her words directly, you would reference it as (Hillier, 2002).
- In both the cases above of direct quote and non-direct citation, you would then need to supply the full bibliographic details for referencing at the end of your written piece. These would need to include author(s), date of publication, title of book, edition (if appropriate), place of publication and name of publisher.
- For journal citations in the text, you should follow a similar format to the one suggested above, though in the references at the end of your piece you would need to include author name, year of publication, title of article, full name of journal, journal number and page of article.
- For electronic references it is best to provide the full web address of the site and if possible the page or section you are referring to.

Summary of key issues covered in this chapter

- How the LLUK standards relate to your professional development.
- Balancing your training needs with those of your employer.
- What counts as professional development from the perspective of the Institute for Learning.
- Evaluating different sources of training and development.
- Maximising learning and reflection potential from externally provided and in-house-led training.
- Maximising learning and reflection potential from self-directed development.
- Managing motivation when carrying out self-directed development.
- Some hints on using the web and simple referencing.

Introduction to Chapters 4, 5 and 6

The following three chapters are devoted to development activities that you could carry out as part of your annual CPD tariff. Below are some general points that apply to all the activities and reflective elements that go with them.

- The activities are meant to be flexible in that you could adapt the ideas and approaches of any one of them to your particular circumstances.
- Alternatively, you could follow any one of them to the letter and you will still come up with an original piece of work since your experience, interpretation and reflection will be yours alone.
- There are no timings imposed and this is deliberate so as to provide the greatest flexibility.
- The domains referred to are taken from the 'New overarching professional standards for teachers, tutors and trainers in the lifelong learning sector'. If you want to view these in greater detail, you will find them on www.lluk.org.uk.
- The domain standards referred to above are: Domain A: Professional values and practice. Domain B: Learning and teaching. Domain C: Specialist learning and teaching. Domain D: Planning for learning. Domain E: Assessment for learning. Domain F: Access and progression. Each activity in the following three chapters indicates at least one domain link.
- Every activity has a small set of reflective tools in the form of prompts or questions that relate to them. It would be advisable to complete all of the questions in the set (usually about five) since that covers the kind of evidence the IfL will need to see.
- There are a range of alternative reflective prompts and questions that you could use if you prefer. They can be found in Chapter 2.
- The depth of reflection is important. Go for the best that your knowledge, experience and motivation can produce. In order to provide enough depth you should aim to write about 100 to 200 words for each reflection response in the set.
- Some of these development activities may involve investigating new aspects or features of practice but many are about deepening or refining the skills and knowledge you already have, perhaps with the help of a fresh approach.
- It is useful to remember that one of the main purposes of this sort of development is to raise the professional profile of the sector as a whole. This process will be enhanced if you undertake to share the knowledge and insight gained from your CPD activities.

Title of activity: Building and maintaining rapport with learners and colleagues

Domain links: A and D

Introduction

Rapport could be said to be the skill of making connections with people in a way that produces comfortable engagement. For you as a practitioner this also means that rapport with your learners is more likely to produce successful learning outcomes. Investigating the skills of initiating and maintaining rapport could also have a positive impact on your work and personal relationships.

An example of rapport would be if you can think of someone that you always feel comfortable with. What signals do you send them and what signal do they convey to you that make you feel this way? How do you use your voice when you talk to them? What are the tone and pace of your speech like? How much eye contact is there? When you smile, how does that affect your voice? What is your posture like when talking to them? How does that all make you feel? If you can answer these questions, you will know what rapport is and what it looks and feels like.

Non-rapport can be unsettling for all concerned and it has particular implications for your role as a teacher, tutor or trainer. When rapport is absent or insufficient, the chances are that learning will be less satisfactory. How do you know when this is the case? What signals do you send out and get back that tells you rapport building is required? It is very likely that most of the positive rapport signals indicated above will be absent or unsystematic.

Rapport is a core skill for life and as a practitioner it is key to being able to positively influence your learners and manage their behaviour. It also helps you to work more effectively with colleagues and it can prevent a lot of the stress that arises from poor communication. To sum up, it is not necessarily about being the life and soul of the party, it is not even about being popular. It is more about adopting flexible behaviour and appreciating differences when dealing with others.

Development brief

Open a file for this activity. Use it to store material, notes and thoughts on the following.

- Start to take a real interest in individuals and what is important to them. Their world is likely to be different from yours. As a teacher, it is useful to have an understanding of the personal perspectives of your learners and what they are feeling. Note down your observations. Think of ways to know your learners better without becoming intrusive.

- Use names frequently when talking to learners and colleagues. It sends a signal that you recognise and value them as individuals and not just as one of the Tuesday afternoon group or one of the course team. Almost everyone responds positively to personal attention. Reflect on how you and your learners respond to the extra emphasis you place on individuals.

- Listen out for some of the key words people use when talking to you. The words they use describe their world as they see, hear and feel it. Use those same words yourself sometimes when responding to them. Avoid using slang or specialist cult language though; subtlety is the key here. When you do communicate using same or similar language, you are exercising your skills of rapport. Note what happens when you do this.

- Make it one of your objectives to notice how individuals prefer to process information and knowledge. Some will need lots of small details to get the idea, others may prefer the big picture first and to fill in the details later. Most will benefit from playing an active part in the learning. For you this means calibrating your teaching strategies and resources to their needs. This is of course, the basis of effective differentiation. Write up one or two effective changes made on the basis of this point.

- Take more note of your own body language and communication skills. Look directly at learners when you are talking. (Many teachers spend too much time looking at the whiteboard, screen or their notes.) Come out from behind your desk. It is a real barrier to communication, not just a physical one. Scan the whole class frequently for signals of understanding and confusion and act on the information you are getting. Invite learner responses rather than pointing at people. Thank them for their contributions using their names. Note down some reflections on this process.

- Locate one or two books or articles about rapport and effective communication. Look at your general notes compiled over three or four weeks and identify briefly how theory could be linked to your experience of developing and maintaining rapport.

- Alternatively, you could keep a regular reflective written or video diary of your experiences in the above areas.

Title of activity: Developing subject resources

Domain links: B and C

Introduction

The best learning resources make use of as many senses as possible. Certainly hearing, sight and kinaesthetic activity can be encouraged to maximise learning, whilst taste and smell also have a key part to play in certain disciplines. Resources are now diverse and often highly professional, even compared to a decade ago. However, technical perfection is not the only factor to guarantee effectiveness. The key to any resource is the extent to which it supports and develops learning for your particular learners and this relies on your understanding of how your learners like to learn. That means all learners, with all their diverse preferences and needs, so the best resources take all these factors into account both in their development and their utilisation.

Development brief

Open a file for this activity. Select a course you teach and within that, a topic that would benefit from the creation of some new resources to support your learners. Spend some time investigating and noting the range of learning needs in your learning group. You may feel able to devise some innovative resources straight away. Perhaps you have been looking for such a opportunity for some time. Many of you, though, might prefer to discuss this issue with colleagues and explore how other people you work with go about creating different devices and activities to increase the potential for learning. As you begin to develop your new resources, bear the following points in mind.

- Don't try to reinvent the wheel. The resource you have in mind may already exist or could be adapted to your needs, so do bit of research first.

- Ask your learners what they need to help them learn more efficiently. If you ask them to tell you what happened in their best learning session to date, you will probably be able to identify some useful ideas.

- Do create different types of resources to meet a variety of learning needs. So you could have some that are mainly visual, such as handouts, illustrations or PowerPoint briefings. Combine these with some that are more auditory-based, such as listening to words or music. (Using the two together may be even more effective.) Have some resources that ask your learners to physically do something, since much of the best learning seems to come from actively applying the theory rather than through the passive absorption of facts. Perhaps ask them to conduct a mini-presentation or act out a role-play.

- Take account of your learners and any specific learning needs that indicate additional support. Do your handouts need to be in a larger font and a clearer typeface? Is the language and the terms you use likely to be understood by everyone? You might also like to consider if any of your resources require differentiated elements for some learners such as extension activities or further examples for those who work at a different pace from average.

- Be innovative. Try something new now and then and evaluate the response from your learners. Devise a game or a quiz to test learning (better still, get your learners to devise one.) Role-play how not to do something; it is much more fun and the learning can be pulled out of the analysis in the feedback.

- When you do create a resource that works, preserve a master copy for future use.

- Share resources and ideas with colleagues. They will be inclined to return the favour and then everyone benefits.

- Review your resources regularly. They may need updating to include new developments and adjusting to meet the needs of different learners.

Once you have devised some appropriate new resources and put a copy of each in your file, you could test them out and evaluate them.

- Test them by introducing one or two at a time into your teaching and noting the way your learners respond.

- Add these observations to your file.

- Devise a way to evaluate your resources, using feedback from learners and a colleague, combined with some self-reflection, and add them to your file.

Title of activity: Developing and analysing a scheme of work

Domain links: A, B, C and D

Introduction

Putting together a scheme of work is often part of the practitioner role and whatever the length of the course, it needs careful planning. Sometimes you might be given a scheme of work that is already prepared. More often though, the task is part of your pre-course preparation. If you have to devise a scheme of work, particularly if it is for something you have not taught before, you could use it to analyse certain aspects of the process as part of your CPD.

Development brief

Open a file for this activity. For the purposes of this exercise we must assume that you have already done the following. If you have not, you could include them as part of the activity.

- Checked the length of the course and how much time you have for each session. This means that you have the number of weeks of teaching and the number of hours clearly defined.
- Identified the desired outcomes of the course. Obtained a copy of the syllabus to identify content or outlined content if no syllabus available.
- Noted assessment modes. Are there exams? If so, who sets them and when and where do they take place? Who will be responsible for marking them? Do the learners have to produce coursework or sit phased tests? When do these need to take place? Do learners have to produce a portfolio? What needs to be in it? How much guidance can you give to learners in their preparation for assessment? All this needs to be clarified before you can properly proceed with planning and if special requirements apply, you would be wise to build them into your plan.

- Identified key dates for the course. Start date, term dates, trips, bank holidays, work experience dates if they apply. Note also any coursework hand-in dates and formal test, presentation and exam dates. You may also have to build in revision sessions, tutorial times and days for individual profiling. Experienced practitioners also know that it is wise to allow time in the first session for ice-breakers and essential administration. The very final session of the course should allow time for learners to provide you with some form of summative evaluation.

- Placed the topics to be taught in logical order to allow for skills development and knowledge building.

Once you are satisfied with the points set out above, you can begin the analysis of your scheme of work by examining and answering the questions below. For your CPD file, it would be wise to add a copy of the syllabus in question, together with a brief outline identifying the nature of the course.

- What research would you need to do to ensure that your subject knowledge for the course content was up to date? Where would you get the information?

- What do you know, and what do you assume about the skills, motivation and experience of your prospective learners? Can any of your assumptions be challenged?

- Devise lesson plans and resources for the first two sessions and briefly explain your rationale for each one.

- Why is the first session particularly important for you and your learners?

- What is you rationale for the order of the topics you plan to teach?

- Explain how informal and formal assessments will contribute to learner outcomes. Identify at least two informal types of assessments that you plan to use regularly and discuss their effectiveness.

- Give at least three examples how you plan to support individual learners as they progress through the course.

- Put all your responses, together with any other relevant material, in your CPD file and add the reflections below.

REFLECTION

- I need to be careful of making assumptions about my future learners because...

- Three new resources I could develop to support learning on this course would be...

- This activity could have a positive impact on my teaching because...

- Is it always true that good planning will ensure a good learning experience? What other factors might be involved?

- Whilst going through this activity an unexpected outcome for me has been...

Title of activity: Exploring professional organisations that support my subject area

Domain links: A, B, C, F

Introduction

Whatever the nature of the subject you teach, you will almost certainly find an organisation or group that exists to share knowledge and practice experience. Some organisations are official bodies dedicated to maintaining standards. Others could be more like special interest forums that rely on contributions from people like you teaching in the life-long learning sector. An advantage of locating and investigating them is that you will come into contact with new people, the latest developments and possibly different perspectives on subjects that you already have some experience of. Most of these organisations now have websites and in many cases they can be accessed without subscription. You could include examining bodies and government sites in your search but remember that there are many non-government sites that offer good support, ideas and subject updating too. This activity can be carried out with groups to maximise the benefits, though it works just as well for the lone researcher.

Development brief

Open a file for this activity.

- Spend some time on the internet investigating as many subject-based organisations as you can. Note down the best ones and write a review of the top six you find.

- If you have colleagues teaching in the same subject area, ask them if they can recommend subject-based organisations that they find useful and follow them up for yourself.

- Investigate two or three of the organisations in more detail by downloading any useful material and following links to other sites that are shown there. Consider registering with the best ones, so that you can get regular updates from them.

- Prepare a briefing suitable for sharing with colleagues that identifies and gives details of the most useful organisations and their sites.

- Write a short piece of around 500 words that shows how you could link aspects of your internet findings to an increasing or updating of your subject knowledge.

REFLECTION

- The most effective sites had the following three main characteristics...

- Being able to access the latest subject information benefits my learners because...

- One thing I feel I could contribute to some of these sites is...

- Being in potential contact with other subject practitioners from all over the world makes me feel...

- Whilst going through this process, I have also learned...

Title of activity: Using reflection as a tool to manage practice issues or problems

Domain links: A, D, F

Introduction

If your practice was always predictable and you rarely needed to question or analyse your interpersonal attitudes and behaviour, there would be less need for this activity. However, practice is not predictable because it involves human beings with differing perspectives on and responses to the same events. This is where the selective use of certain models of reflection could assist you in the process of practice problem-solving. It is important to say, however, that models of reflection do not solve problems. Rather, they can provide you with some tools that encourage reflective thinking and promote constructive action derived from your own unique knowledge about the situation and the individuals involved. It is also useful to say here that the term 'problem' is used loosely to define any practice issue that does not feel right in some way and would benefit from your closer attention.

Development brief

Open a file for this activity.

- Identify the issue or practice problem and set it down in your own words. Talk it through with a trusted colleague or mentor first if that will help you to clarify your thinking and capture the issue as it appears to you.

- Using some reliable source material, identify at least three possible reflective models or approaches that you could employ to help you investigate your issue.

- Explain each model or approach briefly in your own words, taking care to reference properly.

- Apply your issue or problem to each of the models in turn and engage with the processes outlined for each one.

- Evaluate each model as a tool for reflecting on your practice problems and locating solutions. You can do this by discussing the effectiveness of each one in helping to provide you with alternative perspectives and insights.

- Complete your evaluation by suggesting, if appropriate, how each model could be improved.

REFLECTION

- As I see it, the difference between applying reflective models and real-life problem-solving is...

- Applying models to practice problems could help me to...

- The most effective model worked because...

- Sometimes, the underlying assumptions I have about a problem are...

- When I have a professional problem or issue to deal with in future, the first action I could usefully take would be to...

Title of activity: Managing my personal and professional goals

Domain links: A, B, C, E

Introduction

Personal as well as professional goals are included here because they are closely linked. Most of you will have some experience of being involved in annual appraisal or performance review, where former targets, often set with a line manager, are revisited and reviewed and new targets are set for the future. Identifying goals that combine your needs with the needs of your employer are discussed elsewhere in this book, as are setting goals and maintaining motivation over time. This activity is more about identifying and managing your other goals, the ones that may not be identified in a performance review but nevertheless could contribute to your personal and professional confidence and ability. These goals tend to resist being identified as real goals because they are too vague or too negative. 'I want to feel less nervous as a teacher' is not specific enough to work with. Nervous in which way and about what exactly? 'I want to stop teaching "X" because it is too difficult.' Difficult how? What skill or knowledge would make that situation better for you?

This process is good for setting and achieving goals such as greater confidence with aspects of practice, better time management, speaking confidently at meetings, going for promotion or tackling new responsibilities.

Below are some tips for forming goals in a way that might help you.

- Decide exactly what it is that you want. You may have a number of different goals. For the purposes of this activity it may be best to limit them to around three or four.
- Play around with the wording of each goal until you have got a clear and unambiguous description of what it is that you want to have or achieve.
- Note how these goals are becoming objectives and identify, if you can, how they might contribute to the strategic plan of your organisation in some way.
- Check that your goals are all stated in positive terms. You will feel more motivated by, 'I want to look, sound and feel confident when working with...', because it is far more energising than 'I must stop worrying about...'
- Imagine yourself having achieved this goal. What would a more confident you look and sound like? How would you feel? Be really specific. Specifics can turn a goal into an outcome because they can be acted upon because they are clear.
- Remind yourself how you learn best and include those preferences in your plan.
- Identify the steps you need to take in order to reach your goal. Keep each step simple and clearly defined.
- Decide how long you wish each step to take. Be realistic about this; some changes will take longer than others.
- Check to see if you will need any support from a mentor or colleague. Note any resources you are likely to need along the way and secure them before you begin.
- Set a date for taking the first step and take it knowing that you are moving toward something you want.

Development brief

Open a file for this activity.

- Using the above process or a similar resource, identify your goals specifically and plan how you intend to achieve them.
- Set your plan in action and observe the outcomes.
- Keep a reflective diary that charts your progress and your feelings about your development and the impact it has on you and those you work with.

REFLECTION

- I chose this activity because...

- My personal and professional goals are linked because...

- Keeping a reflective diary of my progress has shown me...

- The most interesting change in me has been...

- I could use goal setting with my learners to help them with...

Title of activity: My role in the quality process

Domain links: A, B, C, D, E, F

Introduction

When I was a fairly new practitioner in the sector, I was invited to become a member of the quality committee at my institution. I quickly realised that they weren't saying their committee was better than all the others, they were asking me to get involved with setting and monitoring standards. You may not be pressed into service as a committee member but you will almost certainly play a part in the reporting and maintaining of standards. Most institutions have a series of performance indicators, often with changing annual targets, that are regularly measured, evaluated and debated as part of their quality processes. Performance indicators may differ across institutions, though there are some that appear common to all, such as enrolment, attendance and achievement statistics, probably because of the role they may play in accessing funding. Aspects of your role as a practitioner contribute to quality assurance and quality control as seen here.

Quality assurance is enhanced by the extent to which you:

- participate as a course team member;
- take part in assessment and verification or moderation processes;
- participate in staff development to improve standards of teaching and learning;
- provide learners with access to support;
- evaluate formatively in a valid and reliable manner the courses that you teach and use that feedback to develop your practice;
- take part in regular performance review or appraisal processes.

Quality control pays special attention to:

- final marks and grades achieved in learner outcomes;
- destination surveys that show how learners progress;
- final course reviews and forward action planning;
- reviewing learner outcomes, enrolments and attendance by comparing year-by-year indicators and taking action over unexplained changes in statistics;
- reviewing learner satisfaction via summative survey and taking appropriate actions to ensure future quality.

Development brief

Open a file for this activity.

- Create a chart that illustrates the complete range of quality assurance and control processes active in your institution.
- Indicate clearly the roles that you play in maintaining aspects of quality in your institution.
- Select three of the quality roles you play an active part in and evaluate the effectiveness of each one in terms of their ability to maintain and improve standards.
- Identify an aspect of the quality system in your institution that you currently have no part in and investigate the skills and experience required in order to fulfil that role. If appropriate, part of your investigation could be to shadow someone who currently has responsibility for that area and report your findings.
- Without identifying your institution, suggest a number of ways that the quality provision there could be made even more effective.

REFLECTION

- When I think about quality as a concept, I take it to mean...
- In my view, the most problematic aspect of quality to measure accurately is...
- From my perspective, the most critical performance indicator linked to my practice is...
- Year-on-year comparisons of quality data can sometimes be misleading because...
- It seems to me that the essential differences between quality assurance and quality control are...

Title of activity: Exploring my professional values and behaviour

Domain links: A, E

Introduction

Teaching, training and tutoring in the life-long learning sector carry some fairly serious responsibilities. The quality of the service you provide can affect learner life-chances, particularly in terms of work potential, and you also play a key role as a model for managing interpersonal relationships. Even when you adopt the main principles of andragogy to underpin the way you conduct your professional life, you are still operating from an unequal power position. This is mainly because your learners rely on you to guide them through the unfamiliar world of syllabus interpretation, coursework fine-print requirements and complex assessment procedures. They usually believe that you know more than they do (at least about your specialist area) and that your role includes having the power to assess their work. Therefore, they need you to be consistent, fair, inclusive, informed and focused on their needs as individuals whilst managing them effectively as a group. So it is not surprising if you sometimes feel unclear about the extent and nature of your role as a practitioner and possibly even a bit hazy about the values that underpin your professional motivations. There are two equally useful activities suggested below and you could do either or both, depending on the time you have to give to this development. The first takes a look at your own professional values and drives (recognising of course that they almost certainly emerge from an underlying personal philosophy) while the second is more intent on examining the professional conduct expected of practitioners in the sector as set by the Institute for Learning.

Development brief

Open a file for this activity.

Identifying your professional values

Create a visual representation to examine the issues outlined in the first two points below.

- Teaching is not a career that one usually embarks on by accident. It requires a significant amount of time, planning and effort to gain the subject knowledge and professional skills. Think about what motivated you to undertake such a commitment. What was it about teaching that seemed attractive to you? Why teaching and not another profession? Do you still feel the same now as you did then? What kept you going through the years of training? What particular values emerge from thinking about this issue?

- Having gained the qualifications and secured your post, you have now embarked upon a permanent cycle of professional reflection and development. How does that make you feel? What do you bring to your teaching apart from your knowledge? What does teaching do for you in return? How do you feel when you tell people that you are a teacher? Are any of your personal beliefs and values reflected in the way you see yourself and your role? What keeps you going when the job gets tough?

- Examine the picture or chart you have created. Write a reflective piece on how your values influence your professional behaviour.

- Write a further reflective piece that sums up your feelings about this exercise and discusses the extent to which your personal values are ever compromised or challenged by the demands of your professional role and how you respond.

Identifying the new code of professional practice for teachers in the sector

- Locate and examine the code of professional practice promoted by the Institute for Learning. It is currently in draft form on their website (www.ifl.ac.uk) and will become active in 2008. It aims to set out the standards for professional behaviour and provide a system for the investigation and resolution of any breaches of conduct.

- Produce a report that outlines the format of the document and explains the essential elements in your own words.

- Discuss how you as a practitioner could demonstrate that you comply with the statements on professional values and conduct. Highlight any areas that might prove to be problematic from your perspective.

REFLECTION

- My personal and professional values are...

- Having a professional code of practice makes me feel...

- I became a teacher because...

- When my personal values are challenged by my professional role I...

- My personal and professional behaviour can be a lasting influence on my learners because...

Title of activity: Assessing my work–life balance

Domain link: A

Introduction

The demands of a teaching career can be considerable. Over time, even the most self-aware practitioner can become accustomed to the way professional life tends to spill over into the personal sphere. Once that happens, you are much less likely to question your workload or how you manage it. Some people seem to thrive for years with work commitments that eat into their other life. In fact, that is how workaholics are made. Being conscientious and committed is part of the role but 'Workaholic with no other life' has never, in my experience, featured in the standard practice job description.

It seems that a balance between work and the rest of your world is essential for your physical health, emotional health, your mental well-being and your personal and professional relationships. So how do you assess if you are slipping from healthy, enthusiastic commitment into less healthy, unbalanced obsession?

Look at the statements below and answer them honestly with a simple 'yes' or 'no' or 'sometimes'.

1. I rarely take my lunch break.
2. I take work home with me more than once a week.
3. Thinking about work keeps me awake at night.
4. Colleagues and/or learners have my mobile phone number.
5. I don't take all my holidays most years.
6. Most of my friends work outside education.
7. I have a variety of leisure activities that help me relax.
8. I spend time each week with family and friends.
9. If I am unwell, I would take the appropriate time off.
10. My job is only a small part of who I am.

This is not a scientific survey, but if you said 'yes' to most of the first five statements and 'no' to most of the second five, you may want to consider how healthily balanced your current life is.

Another way to evaluate the relative weight of different aspects of your life is to take the following categories and place a value (Say a figure out 20) on the level of satisfaction you feel with each one as it currently is for you.

- Your home environment.
- Your physical health.

- Your emotional and mental health.
- Your finances.
- Your personal relationships.
- Your leisure time.
- Your personal development.
- Your career.

Development brief

Open a file for this activity.

- Describe, either visually or in your own words, how balanced your work and home life are.
- If it is well balanced, suggest some strategies to keep it that way.
- If it is less well balanced than you would like it to be, produce a visual representation to show how you would like it to be and identify at least two strategies that you could adopt to begin to rectify the situation.
- Act on them and monitor the results for your file.
- Look carefully at your levels of satisfaction completed above and identify at least two simple steps you could take to tackle those each of those areas that you feel are less than optimal for you currently. This does not necessarily mean making big changes all at once to your life, particularly if you bear in mind the 80–20 rule that suggests that 80 per cent of your results come from 20 per cent of your efforts – as long as you apply them in the right direction.
- Keep a simple reflective account of your progress towards a more balanced and satisfactory life.

REFLECTION

- The most useful thing I have learned from doing this activity has been...
- I found that making some of the necessary adjustments made me feel...
- My learners will benefit from the results of this activity because...
- If I was asked to mentor a colleague on managing their work–life balance more effectively, I would suggest they try the following three tactics...
- Having to decide what was really important to me has helped me to...

Title of activity: Writing an article on a professional issue

Domain links: A, B, D

Introduction

Writing an article may seem like an ambitious thing to do if you have never done such a thing before. However, most of you will have written reports and devised written resources that have been made available to an audience of colleagues or learners as part of your role at work. If you look at some of the work-related publications you regularly read, you will see that many of the pieces you read are not necessarily long or over-complicated. In many cases, the best pieces are typified by brevity, clarity and topicality. Explore too the opportunities to write something for a staff journal or compile a briefing for a specialist subject group if you belong to one. If you are keen to submit an article to a journal or specialist publication, it is wise to study it first, so that you are able to produce work in the accepted format and style. Do some research on back copies to familiarise yourself with the sort of content that the editor is likely to be interested in. Most journals prefer you to contact the editor in writing with a brief proposal initially, so you would need to be clear from the outset about the approach and tone you intend to take. Whether you intend to produce a learned piece for a professional journal or an informative or thought-provoking article for the staff magazine, there are some essential points to consider.

- Write about what you know. You have a wealth of experience and knowledge, so share it.
- Avoid lots of jargon. Use straightforward language.
- Prepare your main points before you start and deal with each one in turn.
- Remember the old format for structure: 'Tell them what you are going to tell them. Tell them. Tell them what you have told them'.
- Keep it concise. Some pieces are less than 1000 words and that can be preferable to 3000 words of rambling prose.
- Be as objective as you can. Taking sides too strongly one way or another can look as though you have not really considered all the perspectives.
- Reference properly by acknowledging the work and ideas of others that you use in your writing.
- Check spelling and grammar frequently. If you are not the best proof-reader, get a competent friend or colleague to check it over for you before submitting it.
- Always keep a copy of any work you submit.

Development brief

Open a file for this activity.

- Select three or four outlets for your work that you would like to write for and explore the style and format of each one.
- Discuss them briefly in your file.
- Identify a topic that you know something about and plan how you would structure it for each publication bearing in mind their different audiences.
- Plan, research and write your article in draft form and put it away for at least a week before reading it again. Then read it objectively. Does it say what you meant it to say and in the way you intended?
- Get a friend or colleague to check it for spelling, grammar, flow and coherence. If you are planning to place it for publication in a paper, journal, website or staff publication and this has already been agreed, you could submit it now.
- If you are not yet confident that you have found the correct medium for your work, carry on exploring possibilities such creating your own web page or posting it as a blog.
- If you are not ready to put your work into the public domain yet, remember that the brief for this activity is to write an article, not necessarily to publish it at this stage.

REFLECTION

- Writing an article on a topic I know something about has made me feel...
- I would like to have a piece of my work published in...
- In order to do the above I would need to...
- One other way I could share my knowledge and experience with colleagues would be to...
- Three main criteria for an excellent article are...

Title of activity: Self-assessment of my own teaching skills

Domain links: A, B, C, D, E

Introduction

Assessing your own teaching skills and planning aspects of your own future development is an essential element of professional autonomy. The statements in the development brief below are meant to generate reflection and suggest actions you might like to take for future development. They are neither exhaustive nor exclusive but they do represent a range of criteria whereby you can generally assess your level of teaching skills to date. When you are thinking about each statement, consider the extent to which you are able to carry out a number of these behaviours in the same teaching session, since the combination of these criteria is should be the general aim.

Development brief

Open a file for this activity. With a specific course that you currently teach in mind, reflect and respond to each of the following statements.

- I have a clear scheme of work that is logical and properly structured to meet the needs of my learners and the demands of the subject.
- I have a lesson plan that has properly stated learning outcomes, offers a variety of learning strategies and complementary resources and provides valid forms of assessment and evaluation.
- My records show up-to-date figures for learner attendance and achievement.
- I always share my objectives/learning outcomes for each session with my learners.
- I am confident with my knowledge of the subject I am teaching on this course.
- I like to summarise main learning points as we go along.
- I frequently check on individual and whole-group learning by using a variety of assessment types.
- I emphasise the importance of literacy and numeracy by including both aspects in learning activities whenever possible.
- Health and safety are an important element of my planning and teaching.
- The pace of the session suits all my learners.
- I am comfortable using a range of up-to-date learning technologies.
- I have good rapport with my learners.
- I involve my learners in active learning.
- I use effective strategies to help learners apply their learning to real world situations.

- I use a range of different techniques to summarise main points of the learning at the end of the session.
- My learners are challenged by my teaching approaches.
- My learners are developing autonomy and self reliance due to the strategies I use.

This exercise may take a while to do but it is useful in that it highlights what you are already doing well and allows you to identify areas that might benefit from further attention.

- Identify three main aspects that you feel you do particularly well and outline them. Explain the skills that you are demonstrating when you are doing them.
- Next, identify five aspects from the above list that could be given greater emphasis in your practice than they currently have and show how you plan to implement them more obviously in future sessions.
- If you want to make this into a larger development activity, you could chart the implementation of some or all of the new aspects over a period of time and evaluate the outcomes for you and your learners.

REFLECTION

- Completing this activity has had a positive impact on me and my learners because...
- Before doing this, I may have been making assumptions about...
- Knowing that I already carried out many of the behaviours described in the above statements made me feel...
- One unexpected outcome of this development activity has been...
- My next three goals for further improvement in classroom practice are...

Title of activity: Linking theories and models to my practice

Domain links: A, B

Introduction

If you have ever been asked to do this before, you may recall that it is easier to do in theory than it is in practice. This is because most theory appears as though it were based on a particular case that does not quite apply to your situation. Furthermore, most models or theories, once they are produced in print, imply a certain rigidity and do not lend themselves to manipulation. It is nevertheless a worthwhile exercise to do now and again, if only to remind yourself that a great deal of what you do is at least grounded in some sort of theory that has been formed over time and has been subjected to professional scrutiny from a body of your peers.

A successful activity in this respect would be one that:

- Identifies and outlines some well-chosen and relevant theories that are obviously linked in some way to aspects of your practice. You could, for example, look again at some theory related to adult learning, motivation or memory. No doubt you would have come across some of this in your teacher training.
- Describes clearly how aspects of the theory are linked to your practice by providing specific examples from your recent experience. You might, for example, relate how you applied certain learning strategies in your sessions to facilitate learner recall.
- Evaluates the extent to which theory and practice are linked by discussing what happens to theory when it is applied in a real-life situation.
- Evaluates the extent to which your practice behaviour and professional decisions are influenced by theory.
- Evaluates the extent to which theory is affected and developed by reflection on practice.

Development brief

Open a file for this activity.
- Identify two or three theories that are related to the way you organise and conduct the teaching and learning aspect of your practice.
- Carry out some research on your chosen theories and write them up in your own words, being sure to reference clearly.
- Select some examples from your recent practice to demonstrate how the theory you have selected was implemented in, or contrasted with, your experience of teaching.
- Evaluate, using the evaluation suggestions shown above, the relationship between theory and real-life practice.

REFLECTION

- The most surprising outcome of this activity has been...
- When I think about theory, I now feel...
- One assumption that I used to make about theory that has now changed is...
- Reflection plays a major role in the creation of theory because...
- My practice has some clear links to theory when I look at...

5. Development activities
Planning, delivering, assessing and supporting learning 1

Title of activity: Refining my practitioner skills

Domain links: A, B, C, D, E, F

Introduction

Somewhere in the world of lifelong learning there must exist the model of the perfect lesson. Every practitioner knows however, that even the best models can fail to measure up to the unique demands of individual learners and unforeseen circumstances. It doesn't stop us trying, though. This activity offers a way of analysing some aspects of your current practice with the aim of progressing beyond 'mostly satisfactory' and moving towards 'consistently professional'.

Development brief

Open a file for this activity. Answer the following questions in relation to your current practice. An evaluative sentence or two, plus an example where appropriate, would be better than a yes/no response and help you to plan for developments later.

- I have a detailed scheme of work.
- My lesson plans all have SMART learning outcomes, differentiated activities, show appropriate resources and have clear timings and fair assessment opportunities.
- I note individual learner needs and build them into each session.
- I plan ahead to ensure that I have enough resources and that they are of high quality.
- I always arrive early enough to organise the learning environment to optimise safety and participation.
- I always start the session on time.
- My objectives/learning outcomes are always shared with my learners at the start of the session and reviewed at the end.
- My lesson always begins with a brief recap of learning from the previous session.
- I link learning to learner experience and use up-to-date and relevant examples to show links between theory and real life.
- I always have a variety of learner activities in every session.
- I always offer clear guidance to learners about tasks and activities.

- My body language in the learning environment is assertive, open and encouraging.
- I am comfortable using learner names and use them frequently.
- I always have some differentiated activities and resources available to provide for the individual needs of learners.
- I have a variety of stimulating learning resources and use them to optimal advantage.
- Learning is checked frequently in every session using a wide variety of assessment tools.
- The feedback I give is designed to encourage learners and provides clear advice for further development.
- I like to evaluate each of my sessions once they are finished and take whatever steps I feel are necessary as a result.

Once you have reflected on and answered each of the above questions, you can identify any areas that you feel might benefit from a new approach. Talking your questionnaire responses through with a colleague or mentor could be useful before identifying potential development opportunities.

- Devise a personal development plan that sets out clearly in SMART terms exactly which areas and specific aspects you would like to work on. It is probably best to concentrate on a few aspects and do them well, rather that try to do too much at once. You could phase in certain aspects over time as you develop new skills.
- In your file, keep a reflective journal or video diary of the adjustments you make to your practice, together with some evaluations of the process and outcomes for you and your learners.

REFLECTION

- I chose this activity because I was particularly interested in...
- The most effective adjustment I have made to my practice as a result of this activity was...
- My learners have benefited from this activity because...
- One aspect of my practice that I wish to develop further is...
- The best teaching and learning seems to happen when I ...

Title of activity: Developing new teaching methods

Domain links: A, B, C, D

Introduction

It is all too easy to use the same few teaching and learning methods again and again because they seem to work and the learners like them. However, sometimes methods that have become too safe and comfortable are less effective than those that provide variety and an element of novelty. Below is a list of teaching methods that you could try or adapt to your teaching circumstances. The list is by no means exhaustive, so if you have other methods you have always wanted to explore, you could incorporate them into this activity.

Lecture	Seminar
Buzz-group	Simulation
Discussion – whole group	Make a video
Discussion – small group	Practical workshop
Demonstration and copy	Quiz (teacher devised)
Demonstration and class review	Quiz (learner devised)
Demonstration – spot the errors	Guest speaker
Field trip	Completing gapped handout
Role-play (how to do it)	Research and feedback
Role play (how not to do it)	Board blast/thought shower
Group project	Case study
Individual project	Presentations
Question and answer	Mind-mapping
Learner as teacher	

Development brief

Open a file for this activity and keep notes of your progress in the form of a reflective diary.

- Select two or three methods that you do not currently use.
- Explore (perhaps by discussing with a colleague or mentor) how you could incorporate one or more of them into a number of future lessons.
- If possible, ask to observe a colleague who is using this method and reflect on how you could adapt their approach to your own learners. New methods often mean that you will need to devise some careful briefings for learners or new resources to support the experience, so give yourself time to prepare ahead.

- Introduce the new methods into some of your lessons and carry out an evaluation at the end of each one. Your evaluation should include your own reflections and suggestions for further adjustments, plus some feedback from your learners.

REFLECTION

- The main advantages and disadvantages of the methods I introduced were...

- When I reflect about the way I teach, I think I use certain methods and not others because...

- Developing some new teaching approaches has made me feel...

- The main component of the most effective teaching and learning approaches seems to be...

- Three other teaching methods I would like to introduce in the future are...

Title of activity: Putting the behaviour into SMART learning objectives

Domain links: A, B, C, D, E

Introduction

Sometimes it is useful to remind yourself about the importance of having clearly defined learning outcomes. The learning outcomes or objectives of any session need to be clear in the sense that you and your learners will be able to tell when they have been achieved. They also need to be valid in the sense that they express the correct level of skill required in terms that are understood by everyone concerned. It helps, when setting out learning outcomes or objectives, to remember that each one should be prefaced with the actual or implied phrase:

'By the end of the session, the learner should be able to...'

This means that your learning outcomes or objectives are stated as verbs or words that describe behaviour because this way it is clear if the learner has achieved them or still has more work to do. Therefore properly written learning outcomes or objectives provide you and your learners with a clear structure for each learning session and also enable you to evaluate the extent of the learning once the session is at an end.

Development brief

Open a file for this activity. Look at the behavioural terms shown below. They are listed in order of their relative skill or difficulty. They are meant to be an indication of the sort of terms it is helpful to use for setting objectives or learning outcomes when you want learners to be able to demonstrate differing skills and abilities.

Simple behavioural terms demonstrating knowledge

- List
- Define
- State
- Outline
- Describe
- Label
- Identify
- Select

Simple behavioural terms demonstrating comprehension

- Explain
- Adjust
- Give examples
- Paraphrase
- Discuss
- Summarise
- Translate
- Generalise

Medium-level skill behavioural terms demonstrating application

- Demonstrate
- Develop
- Calculate
- Estimate
- Convert
- Plan
- Produce
- Construct
- Predict
- Prepare
- Manage
- Solve

Medium-level skill behavioural terms demonstrating analysis

- Rationalise
- Differentiate between
- Identify factors
- Assess
- Review
- Interpret
- Relate
- Contextualise
- Argue for and against
- Link theory to practice

High-level skill behavioural terms demonstrating synthesis

- Draw together
- Combine
- Create your own version
- Generate
- Design an alternative
- Modify
- Encapsulate
- Link

High-level skill behavioural terms demonstrating evaluation

- Appraise
- Justify
- Compare
- Contrast
- Weigh up
- Evaluate
- Discriminate between
- Critically reflect on

- Identify at least four previously taught sessions that would have been improved by rewording your objectives or learning outcomes to approximate the skills levels indicated above.
- Discuss how changing the wording could have potentially improved each session for you and your learners.
- Plan your next four sessions, stating your objectives clearly in behavioural terms that match the skills level you require. After you have taught them, review each session, paying particular attention to the extent to which learning outcomes were met.
- Put together a file containing the four previously taught sessions and your analysis of them, showing the changes you made and why. Add the four sessions with behavioural objectives you subsequently devised and your analysis of their outcome. Contribute any further behavioural terms that you plan to use in the future that relate particularly to your subject area.

REFLECTION

- Clear and valid learning outcomes or objectives mean that my learners...
- Using behavioural objectives helps me to plan...
- When setting behavioural objectives I need to take account of...
- I would use a range of behavioural terms from different levels in some sessions because...
- This activity has links to theory by...that argues...

Title of activity: Seven of the best: Innovating my teaching strategies

Domain links: A, B, C, D, E

Introduction

Even when you employ a range of different methods to teach your learners, the chances are that there are still some innovative approaches you could try. The ones shown below have been selected because they are adaptable to many subject areas. More importantly, they feature an active and sometimes multi-sensory approach to learning that accelerates the learning process for many participants.

You could use them in combination or just employ one or two in each session.

- **Use some music in the session**. Use it for entrances and exits. Use it for changes between topics or activities. Use it to aid concentration. Use it to signify a change of pace. Use it to aid relaxation during small-group work. Obviously you will need to check that you have the necessary permission to play recordings and it is best to avoid lyrics since they can be distracting.

- **Tell them stories**. Metaphors and stories are a good way of getting learning across without being too obvious. It is a way of making suggestions and posing solutions without actually having to tell people what to do. The theory is that 'stories' work directly on the unconscious mind and the lesson to be learned from the story is absorbed and adapted according to the listener's model of the world. I have found this approach very useful when teaching new teachers. I would tell them true 'stories' about the mistakes I made when new to the profession and what I did to try and put them right. Often we would laugh at how naïve I had been but the point of the story meant that the likelihood of my learners making the same errors was substantially reduced because they had learned from my experience. Use stories also to illustrate case studies; use them to help learners solve problems. You could also help learners to create their own stories to help each other.

- **Go multi-sensory**. There is a lot of evidence to suggest that the more senses involved in learning, the more likely it is that the learning will be retained. Make the most of visual props by accentuating colour and contrast, use your voice in a variety of ways and employ other sound sources such as music and vocal contributions from your learners. Have activities that involve learners in moving around such as role play or mini-presentations and you will notice that they tend to stay more alert. If they are more alert, they are more likely to be learning.

- **Put in lots of mini-breaks and changes of activity**. Most people's brains benefit from a short break from learning about every 45 minutes. It doesn't have to involve leaving the learning environment or having a cup of tea. A brain break can be instigated by a change of activity. You could try switching from a passive activity to an active one for example or re-forming groups along different lines. Another tactic is to set a problem to solve and then have a five-minute break or change of focus before resuming. This allows learners' brains to filter the problem and have time to think before having to 'perform'.

- **Use concept maps to aid recall**. Most people remember what they have seen more readily than what they have heard. Similarly, there is a lot of evidence to suggest that carrying out a task enables learning with understanding. If you want learners to remember with understanding, you could ask them to produce a concept map or similar visual representation of their learning so far in the session. Concept maps are also good for identifying the connections between concepts. So draw concept maps to illustrate your ideas when you are teaching and get your learners to produce their own versions to show what they have learned.

- **Use a mix of right- and left-brain activities in each session**. Include a range of activities in every session to suit left- and right-brain preferences. Left-brain preferences include verbal descriptions, linear progression of ideas, analysis that breaks things down in order to understand them and a leaning towards facts. Right-brain learners tend to prefer tasks that ask them to 'see' links between factors. They tend to like pictures and visual reinforcement and prefer to synthesise (join things together) rather than analyse. So arrange learning activities that optimise their best skills as well as challenge their less preferred ones.

- **Get your learners to recap, sum up and look forward at the close of the session**. Many teachers revisit their objectives at the end of the session. It may be better for your learners, in terms of 'fixing' their learning, if you ask them to do it and also ask them to show briefly what and how they have learned using visual, verbal and active behaviour. Another group could identify links between what has been covered that day and what will be addressed in the next session.

Development brief

Open a file for this activity.

- Select one or more of the innovations described above and incorporate them into a few of your learning sessions. It is best to introduce one new approach at a time so that you can judge the effect more clearly. Alternatively, you could phase in all of the suggestions above into your sessions over a period of weeks.

- Using your own version of a reflective diary or blog, write about what you chose to do and how you went about it and the response you got from your learners and how you felt about it.

- Put it all together with some underpinning evidence or theory to support the innovations you implemented. You will find a lot about accelerated learning techniques on the internet.

REFLECTION

- If I were to co-mentor a colleague, the three most effective strategies I would recommend to accelerate learning potential in the classroom would be...

- One aspect of accelerated learning that I wish I understood better is...

- When I was trying some of these different approaches I realised that...

- One new idea I wish to introduce in the future is...

- Innovating my teaching strategies has had an effect on my learners in that...

Title of activity: Dealing with deletion, generalisation and distortion in communication

Domain links: A

Introduction

Bandler and Grinder published a book in 1975 called *The Structure of Magic*. They were not aiming to teach you how to do card tricks but how to analyse and clarify language in order to help the communication process. This is a skill that has endless applications in your role as a practitioner. You need others to understand you, and you want to be able to comprehend fully what others are trying to convey.

Bandler and Grinder suggested that people use language specifically to represent their experience of the world and this tends to lead to language being selected that deletes, generalises or distorts reality.

- **Deletion** is typified by people omitting detail when they speak or through ignoring detail when listening. When this happens, information given or received tends to be vague.
- **What can you do about deletion?** You can always ensure that you provide enough context and detail when communicating and you can use questioning to clarify deletion in others. Ask learners for more detail when they make vague statements.
- **Generalisation** is a useful skill. It enables us to extrapolate our thinking and learning from one event to other similar events and learn from the experience. However, it can work against us if the thinking is used to generalise from one negative example. This leads to a fair bit of 'disaster' language and thinking such as 'I always fail this sort of test', 'I am rubbish at exams', or 'They never pick me for the team'. It can also tend to lean towards unhelpful and generally negative thinking about certain groups of people in society in a way that is close to prejudice.
- **What can you do about generalisation?** Challenge it gently when you hear it. When you hear words like always, everyone, never, nobody, can't and must, you can respond by questioning if that statement is really true in all circumstances. Usually generalisations can be successfully challenged. 'I can't' can be met with 'Who says so? What stops you? What would happen if you did?' Be cautious about generalising when talking to learners. It is useful to them to learn to appreciate that there are often exceptions to generalised statements which challenge their validity.
- **Distortion.** Have you ever been involved in an incident or event where everyone has a differing recollection of what happened? Have you ever discussed a book you have read and found others had interpreted it completely differently? Distortion happens because events are experienced through everyone's individual filters and those filters are influenced by our personal life experiences and the way we have learned to respond to them.

83

So an event may appear more serious than it is, or distortion may lead you to interpret the behaviour or motivations of others in a way that was not intended. Because it is part of who we are, distortion is tricky to spot in others and tough to challenge in our own behaviour.

● **What can you do about distortion?** Listen for language, either your own or from other people, that either makes too much or too little of an experience. Distorting can add events that didn't happen or underplay those that did. Distorted interpretation can lead to making assumptions that are not true but feel real. Challenge the language and the thinking, gently.

Development brief

Open a file for this activity.

● Carry out an investigation into the aspects of communication discussed above. Identify some theory about how deletion, generalisation and distortion can affect the language we use and how we think. Put it in your own words.

● Outline the possible consequences of habitually thinking in a deleted, generalised or distorted manner.

● Produce a case-study style presentation to inform your colleagues about the nature of deletion, generalisation and distortion and how they can recognise it, in their own behaviour and in relation to their learners and take steps to deal with it.

● If you wish to and are able to, you could deliver your presentation and manage a discussion afterwards. Put a copy of your presentation and any evaluatory feedback in your file.

REFLECTION

● Challenging deletion, generalisation and distortion in myself and others has shown me...

● The link between the way people think and the way they behave is...

● Challenging distorted and generalised thinking is a bit like challenging assumptions because...

● One book I could read that would tell me more about this is...

● One change I have noticed in my own language and thinking since looking at this issue is...

Title of activity: Developing strategies to support learners with specific learning difficulties

Domain links: A, B, C, D, E, F

Introduction

Any group you teach is likely to manifest a variety of learning needs. A bit of thought and some careful planning can meet a range of needs including some that indicate specific learning support needs such as dyslexia and similar difficulties. Below are a number of strategies you could utilise in any learning session. It is important though to remember that every learner is different and some will respond positively to certain strategies and others will not, so the most important thing to do first is involve them. Ask them what works for them in this sort of situation because they are the expert, at least as far as their own preferences are concerned. You could try some of the strategies set out below and ask for feedback and adjust your approach accordingly. This sort of activity potentially benefits all your learners, since everyone tends to appreciate clarity.

Development brief

Open a file for this activity. Below are nine strategies you could employ to support learners with specific learning difficulties. Select a few at a time, beginning with those that seem the most appropriate and introduce them into your teaching. Create activities that enable all learners to demonstrate their understanding or skill by the end of the session.

1. Print handouts and devise PowerPoints with pale-coloured backgrounds. Keep all visual resources as clear and uncluttered as you can.

2. Link all your present teaching to previous learning and achievements. This provides context, aids recall and can increase confidence.

3. Use charts, concept maps, diagrams and other visual representations to supplement written handouts.

4. Keep written handouts to key points only with print size 14 or 16 and use uncomplicated fonts. Make use of bold and underline functions to emphasise key points. Use bullet points rather than continuous prose.

5. Break down all learning activities into smaller sequences. Talk them through the whole process and check understanding before starting. Always ensure that a written version of the activity remains visible for those who have difficulty processing the details of time-ordered tasks.

6. When teaching a new concept, use a number of real-life examples that learners can identify with. If you cannot find real-life examples, tell them a story that illustrates how the concept works using scenarios they would be familiar with.

7. Write all new words on the top left of the whiteboard in clear lettering. Use black markers to aid those with red–green recognition problems. Box it or underline it to emphasise it and say it out loud and explain what it means.

8. Use language to signpost different aspects of the lesson: 'This leads me to...' 'The next set of ideas are a complete contrast...' 'Before break we need to look at...' Use your voice to emphasise important points and write them down at the same time.

9. Use verbal questioning to assess some learning. Written assessments could sometimes take the form of gapped handouts. Lots of learning can be demonstrated through presentations, quizzes and role plays.

For your file, say why you have selected certain strategies and why you think they may be useful for your learners. Keep a copy of relevant lesson plans and write up an evaluation of each strategy that includes some reflection from you, some feedback from your learners and any research you find that supports or questions these approaches.

REFLECTION

- One further strategy I would like to try is...
- I would like to know more about...
- The strategies I used in this activity potentially helped all my learners because...
- The most important thing I have learned by doing this is...
- The most interesting theory that I came across in relation to the activity above was...

Title of activity: Examining assessment to improve learner outcomes

Domain links: A, B, C, D, E

Introduction

Most learning on courses is assessed, so one of the most important skills learners should develop is a clear understanding of the assessment criteria and how the assessment outcomes are arrived at. Of course, this is particularly an issue for learners on courses where their work is graded in some way. They may be assessed against pass, merit and distinction criteria. Others have to interpret literal grades such as A, B or C (or worse still, A–, B+ and C–). Yet others are left wondering what 18 out of 25 actually means and some have to try to grasp the real implications of their latest percentage mark when it has gone up or down by a few points since the last assessment.

This activity assumes that the grading system you use is valid. That is, that it mirrors the overall assessment pattern and is consistently applied throughout the course.

One of the most positive approaches to helping learners to appreciate just what their course assessment grades actually mean is to set up a session that involves them directly in assessing the sort of work they are likely to produce themselves. Once they have examined closely how the material is related to the grade criteria, they are much more likely to be able to produce their own assignments to an improved level. Furthermore, any anxiety about grade performance is reduced by working on the anonymous assignments rather than their own. Learners do not need to be highly able or knowledgeable to do this exercise. They do need to be able to tell the difference between a good piece of work and a poor one and be able to say why.

This activity does require some preparation.

- You would need to identify at least five pieces of work, of varying grades, ranging from high marks through to refer/fail, completed by learners in a previous year. It would be important, however to ensure that the course and the assessment criteria were the same as currently used by your learners.
- Remove any identifiers from the past assignments, such as names or tutor groups.
- Remove the assessment grades and comments given by the assessor.
- Copy the pieces of work, so that every learner in your session has access to all five assignments.
- Provide clear and current assessment criteria that identify the standards of work required for each grade.

Development brief

Open a file for this activity.
- Set up the exercise for your learners as shown above.
- Get the learners to read the provided assignments on their own and, using the current assessment criteria, tentatively apply a grade and comments to each one. You need to give them enough time to do this properly.
- Ask them to work in small groups to compare their findings and discuss the reasoning behind the grades they gave.
- Ask each group to agree grades for each of the assignments and provide a brief feedback on each one that justifies their decision.
- During whole-group feedback at the end, you can tell them the actual grade that was given and verified for each assignment. If there are any major discrepancies in their assessments compared to the real ones, you can clarify issues for them.
- In your file, supply the details of the activity you have conducted with your learners.

- Evaluate the session using learner feedback and your own reflection. Your reflection could include a discussion about what was going on in this process that helped learners to comprehend the finer points of grading standards and why that knowledge can potentially improve future work.

- Later, you may be able to discuss the extent to which the exercise has produced any improvement to learner confidence and assignment grades.

REFLECTION

- The most important outcome of this activity for my learners has been...

- Doing this activity has taught my learners more than just how to improve their grades because...

- My understanding of the assessment processes I use has developed because...

- The hardest part of this activity for my learners was...

- Next time I do this activity, I could make it even more effective by...

Title of activity: Forming groups and facilitating effective group work

Domain links: A, C, D, E

Introduction

You may sometimes find it difficult to ask adults to get into groups. However, if you always allow them to decide their own group compositions, you will probably end up with the same groups each time and the potential for real interactive learning is reduced. Learners need variety, even if they are a little wary of it, so you could use the techniques shown here to allocate learners to different groups from the ones they would normally opt for. You will also find below some statements about the way group work could be facilitated. If you examine each one, you could identify any strategies that you might like to add to your current approaches and having introduced them, evaluate the outcome for this file.

- **Mixed ability and learning preferences**. You would need time to review this before the session began and have the groups already formed on paper. You would need to know the learners, their capabilities and learning style preferences in order to 'layer' the group to ensure a range of skills and approaches in each one.

- **Birthday groups**. In any large class, you could ask them to form groups on the basis of their birth month and adjust any groups that are too large by splitting them or combining any that are too small.
- **Geography**. Select groups on the basis of their current seating arrangements. This tends to be fast and straightforward, so is good for short periods of group work and minimises disruption in crowded rooms. It reduces shyness, since most learners will already be sitting in a place of their choice. It does, however, produce similar groups each time because learners tend to sit in the same seats for each session, with the outcome alluded to above.
- **Lucky dip**. Decide how many groups you want. (For the sake of this exercise let us assume five groups are needed.) Prepare enough sticky labels or cards in advance with one of five symbols on and ask each member of the group to select a label or card at random. Ask them to search the class to find the rest of the group holding the same symbol and introduce themselves.
- **Number groups**. If you want to have five groups, go round the whole class and point to each person whilst saying a number. For five groups you would say, one, two, three, four, five and again one, two, three, four, five, until you had given everyone a number between one and five. Then, you would ask all the ones to form a group and all the twos to form a group and so on. This method mixes groups up quite well and provides learners with the opportunity to work with someone who does not usually sit near them.

Facilitating group work can be done by:

- outlining clearly the nature of the group task and providing written learning outcomes for reference;
- being clear about what you expect them to do and how long they have to do it;
- checking for understanding before commencing;
- giving them time to think, plan and organise themselves;
- building in a break if possible;
- asking for interim feedback from each group during the process to ensure that everyone is participating;
- asking questions instead of telling them what to do, 'What will you do next?' is more facilitative than giving orders or advice before it is really needed;
- encouraging reflection from learners on the process as well as the product – this enables them to evaluate their team roles in addition to the work produced.

Development brief

Open a file for this activity.

- Read up and implement some of the group-forming strategies suggested above.

- Review and record the results for your file. You may wish to gather some feedback from your learners about their reactions to this new approach and add some of your own reflective evaluations.

- Examine the suggestions for facilitating group work shown above, and either demonstrate using a typical learning session how you already do this, or introduce any missing elements into your group work sessions and evaluate the outcomes.

REFLECTION

- Being more proactive about getting my learners into groups made me feel...
- My preferred group-forming technique is...because...
- Helping learners to be effective group workers will have an impact on...
- I can find theory to support the tactics I use by looking at...
- The next aspect of group management I would like to tackle is...

Title of activity: Developing mentoring skills

Domain links: A, B, D, E

Introduction

The benefits of having access to a good mentor are well known. Less appreciated are the benefits of being a mentor to fellow colleagues. This activity explores both these possibilities. However, do remember that this is not a mentor-training activity, though after completing it you may be in a better position to assess your suitability for the role and put a case for some training to your line manager.

The role of the mentor is to:

- support colleagues in all aspects of their practice;
- be a critical friend when necessary;
- help colleagues to identify and manage their development goals;
- observe colleagues in the learning environment when requested and provide constructive feedback;
- guide mentees towards finding their own solutions to professional problems.

Mentors need to be:

- consistently professional in their practice;
- a good role model for others;
- sensitive, approachable and supportive;
- available, within reason;
- knowledgeable and up to date in their subject area;
- conversant with and able to use reflective practice models;
- confident and capable managers of learning;
- observant and analytical;
- able to give written and verbal constructive feedback to colleagues;
- trustworthy – they need to know when to keep a confidence;
- reliable – part of being a professional is doing what you say you will do.

Being a mentor to others:

- promotes a personal increase in reflection and self-evaluation;
- brings focus – if you want to learn something really well, teach it to someone else;
- offers a potential increase in job satisfaction;
- is a valuable skill to add to your CV;
- gives you professional status and recognition;
- can form part of your CPD process;
- can be seen as experiential learning with the opportunity to learn a whole set of new skills.

Having a mentor yourself could help you to:

- develop and hone all your practice skills;
- develop your subject knowledge;
- network more effectively;
- model professional behaviour;
- identify new development goals and manage them efficiently;
- gain confidence and develop autonomy.

Development brief

Open a file for this activity.

- Reflect on the benefits of having (or theoretically having) a mentor to support you in your development as a practitioner. Identify and explain a specific incident where you think that mentor support would have been desirable.

- Go through the 'role of the mentor' as shown above. Go on to examine the 'mentor needs to be' section. For each point, reflect carefully and comment on the extent to which you feel you have the necessary characteristics to be a mentor.

- Identify the areas where you would most need to develop your skills in order to become a mentor.

- Contact a mentor and arrange an informal discussion with them. Ask them about the benefits and disadvantages of the role and use their feedback together with the section 'being a mentor to others' to reflect in writing on the future possibility of mentor training.

- You could also, if you are motivated towards mentorship, discuss the possibility of mentor training with a line manager and ask for it to be included in your professional aims for performance review. It may help your case if you have identified some training sources and can outline to your manager the likely benefits of you developing these skills.

REFLECTION

- Good mentors need to be able to...

- I think I have many of the qualities described to make a good mentor but I still need to develop...

- My ideal mentor would...

- One aspect that concerns me still about the mentor system is...

- State three ways that being a mentor could enhance your own practice.

Title of activity: Helping learning groups to work more effectively in teams

Domain links: A, B, C, D

Introduction

If you use learner-centred approaches, you probably include group work among your regular teaching and learning strategies. If this is the case, you may find that group work produces variable outcomes depending on the personalities in each team. If you want to increase the effectiveness of group work in your practice, you could begin by helping learners to appreciate the nature of group dynamics and team roles in relation to their activities. This is not usually time wasted, since group work, team efficiency and the quality of outcomes tend to improve once learners have had the opportunity to explore some theory in relation to their experiences as team members. There are a number of theories you could use. Tuckman (1965), for example, identified four stages of group development:

- **Forming**: Describes the way the group first comes together. The purpose is defined and terms of reference agreed.
- **Storming**: As the group gets to know each other, individuals begin to exert their views. This stage can include disagreements, changes of roles and challenges to the original terms of reference.
- **Norming**: At this point, the conflicts lessen, the group have established their standards and norms of behaviour and they can focus on what they need to do.
- **Performing**: The team at this stage has sufficient stability and sense of purpose to work effectively as a team towards a common purpose.

In 1977, in conjunction with Jensen, Tuckman added a further stage:

- **Adjourning**, to describe the way teams deal with the end of a project and the dissolution of the team identity.

In terms of team roles, you could explore Belbin's work (1996) and introduce it to your learners to help them identify their preferred approaches and the skills they need to develop in order to become effective team members.

Following any group work that takes place once the concepts have been introduced, you could increase the learning for the participators by conducting a brief plenary session that addresses questions such as:

- What skills did your team need to have in order to complete this task?
- How were the roles allocated?
- Individually, are there skills you have observed in your fellow team members that you would like to develop?
- What role or roles did you play according to Belbin's model?
- From your experience, is Tuckman right about the stages groups go through?

Development brief

Open a file for this activity.

- Using the references above and the internet, explore some models and theories related to team development and team roles. Outline them for your file.
- Introduce the concept of Belbin's team roles to your learners by explaining the theory briefly and inviting them to identify and evaluate the team roles they are likely to adopt when working groups.
- Introduce the concept of group development and outline at least one theory, such as Tuckman's (1977), that accounts for the way groups come together and manage projects and tasks to completion.

- Next time you set any group work, remind your learners about group development and team roles and ask them to take note of their behaviour in that respect.
- Once the group work has come to an end, conduct a plenary session (see above for some ideas) that invites your learners to discuss issues relating to their group formation and individual roles.
- Write up for your file a reflective account of the way your learners have responded to the incorporation of team roles and group formation into their activities.

REFLECTION

- Learning about group development and roles has helped my learners to...
- Appreciating group dynamics should benefit my learners beyond the classroom because...
- Identifying the roles they play in groups has given learners...
- If I were to suggest any criticism of the theories I used, it would be...
- Thinking about group development and roles has helped me to appreciate my own behaviour when...

Title of activity: Becoming more learner-centred in my teaching strategies

Domain links: A, B, C, D, E

Introduction

It is fairly common to see teachers managing learning by placing themselves physically at the front of the class and orchestrating their whole session while standing over their learners and revealing their wisdom a bit at a time. It is probably how you remember being taught yourself and it may seem a natural approach to take given the implied relationship dynamics of the course, namely, you are the expert and they are present to learn what you know. Being 'in-charge' this way also can be a comfort if you worry about control issues. Perhaps if you give your learners too much choice, they will choose to pay you less attention and show you less respect. This mindset tends to result in a teacher-centred approach to classroom practice and when this is the case you will often note the following characteristics:

- the teacher is the main focus for the learner rather than the learning;
- the learning begins and ends when the teacher says so;
- the teacher 'gives' information to learners at a rate and quantity controlled by them as the provider of knowledge;

- teaches what the teacher has decided, irrespective of learner needs;
- tends to provide information in large quantities but less in the way of activities for learner discussion and analysis;
- the learners tend to be passive, with low levels of participation;
- creates a 'parent–child' dynamic that may encourage dependency in learners.

By contrast, learner-centred approaches tend to display the following traits:

- the learner and their individual learning needs are the focus of the process;
- learning to learn is as important as memorising facts;
- the teacher uses learner experience to optimise learning;
- learners are encouraged to seek out information for themselves;
- learners are encouraged and supported in the development of their skills of reflection, interpretation and evaluation;
- learning is something the learner does rather than has done to them;
- the teacher becomes a facilitator rather than the leader;
- the learner is able to develop autonomy and independence.

Development brief

Open a file for this activity.

- Carry out an investigation of available literature that relates to andragogy and summarise at least two theories in your own words.
- Carry out a self-audit, using the factors identified above, to reflect and evaluate your current approach to teaching and learning.
- Devise a plan to introduce more learner-centred approaches into your teaching and introduce them gradually, evaluating the outcomes as you go.
- Discuss as you see it, using examples where appropriate, the reality of applying andragogical theory in practice.

REFLECTION

- The difference between the theory of andragogy and what happens in practice is...
- Sometimes, I feel that my teaching and learning approaches are...
- The most interesting theory I came across suggested that...
- Three teaching methods that I could use that reflect the andragogical approach are...
- Learner-centred approaches enable a greater sense of learner autonomy because...

Title of activity: Putting CLASS into lesson design

Domain links: A, B, C, D, F

Introduction

When you consider the number of classes you need to devise in any one year, it is not surprising if sometimes they seem to fall short in some small indefinable way. All the ingredients seem to be present yet the chemistry fails to work.

Try applying the CLASS test to your lesson plans before you implement them. If they are found wanting in any respect, you can insert the missing element for a more positive outcome. Your learners will tend to have a better learning experience and you should feel more profession as a result. The CLASS test says every lesson should be:

- **Challenging** to learners. Not beyond their abilities but stretching their knowledge and skills enough to be invigorating.
- **Linked** to what they already know or have experience of. Build on their existing knowledge and understanding when introducing new concepts. Compare or contrast the new concepts with recent or previous learning and show how the ideas are related.
- **Action** or activity-based. Build a number of different activities into every session so that every learner can participate by doing, as well as looking and listening.
- **Structured** clearly. All tasks should be structured clearly, so each learner is clear about their role, how much time they have, what they need to do and why. The way you introduce concepts also needs to have a logical structure. What skills or knowledge do they need to already possess before they tackle this next stage?
- **Supported** by resources that meet different learning needs. Who is likely to need more explanation or examples and how can you provide them? Who will need extra support with basic skills and how can you secure it? Have you got resources that will stretch the faster learners and keep them motivated? Are the resources that you intend using sufficiently diverse to satisfy a range of learning style preferences?

Development brief

Open a file for this activity.

- Take a series of recently taught lesson plans and subject them to the CLASS test.

- Show where you would make adjustments now to meet the CLASS criteria.
- Devise at least four new lesson plans that comply with the CLASS model.
- Deliver the new lessons using CLASS criteria and reflectively evaluate each one thoroughly.

REFLECTION

- I chose this development activity because...
- The effects of implementing CLASS criteria in my lesson plans have been...
- One further criterion I would like to add is...
- An example of how CLASS criteria can be related to certain learning theories is...
- The most useful part of this activity has been...

Title of activity: Exploring student-centred assessment links to andragogy

Domain links: A, C, D, E

Introduction

Assessment often feels like something that is 'done to' learners rather than done for them. This development activity looks more closely at how to involve learners fully in the assessment process. When learners are placed at the centre of the process, many of the operational principles of andragogy become closer to reality, so this is an opportunity to demonstrate how to turn theory into practice.

Below are a number of ways you could involve your learners more directly in their learning and show them that they are partners in the assessment process.

- Explain the nature of the assessment criteria clearly before they start and give examples if necessary.
- Ensure that any verbal explanation is accompanied by written support.
- Use strategies that provide opportunities for learners to assess their own work against the assessment criteria.
- Create exercises that enable learners to assess some 'model answers' you have created against the assessment criteria they will have to work to. Getting learners to mark and assess work this way helps them to understand the differences between grade boundaries and shows them examples of good, average and poor responses.
- Use strategies that allow learners to peer assess some of their work and show them how to provide and make use of constructive feedback.
- When you are about to give some verbal feedback, invite the learner to tell you first, how they rate the work in question.
- Ask learners to state ways in which their work could be improved and build their responses into your feedback.
- Be specific about the details of your praise and criticism.
- Finish your feedback by inviting them to focus on future performance.

Development brief

Open a file for this activity.

- Investigate at least two theories related to andragogy and summarise them for your file.

- Create a case study that uses one of your learning groups to identify ways in which you could demonstrate some of the principles of andragogy in the way you conduct assessments.
- Begin to introduce some of the assessment strategies shown in the list above and evaluate the outcomes for you and your learners.

REFLECTION

- I can show how at least one theory about andragogy relates to the way I prefer to conduct assessments by citing...

- One aspect of andragogical theory I wish I understood better is...

- The impact of this activity on my learners has been...

- I could extend andragogical principles to other areas of my teaching by...

- Involving my learners fully in the assessment process is important because...

Title of activity: How effective is my feedback to learners?

Domain links: A, B, C, D, E

Introduction

In order for learners to learn in the most effective way, they need to know how well they are doing as they go along. The quality of the feedback you provide as part of the management of their learning is critical to this process. Feedback can be a key motivator when done well. Equally it can be a demoralising experience to receive poor-quality or negative feedback that fails to offer constructive advice on how to improve. Look at the statements below related to feedback and identify those that you know you always do well and those that you still need to do some further work on.

- I turn every assessment into a learning opportunity for learners.
- I often ask learners to rate their own work against the assessment criteria before I see it.
- I use self-assessment and peer assessment with learners in order to balance out the teacher-centred nature of most feedback.
- I aim to give written and/or verbal feedback as rapidly as possible after the assessment event.
- The feedback I give is objective in that it relates to the work in question rather than the personality of the learner.
- I always outline what has been done well as well as what needs improving.

- Whenever I can, I show examples of the desired outcome, if work needs improving.
- The feedback I give relates closely to the wording of the assessment criteria.
- I avoid over-praising or over-critical language in written and verbal feedback.
- My feedback often includes new targets to develop learning.
- I use positive language such as, 'You can improve this piece of work by...'
- I always personalise feedback by using learner names.

Development brief

Open a file for this activity. There are two activities you could do here. Either do both or consider covering one aspect in greater depth.

- Work with a colleague to examine the way you each currently provide written and verbal feedback for at least one set of learners. Provide examples of written feedback given recently to learners in relation to either formal or less formal assessments. For each example provided, offer some written discussion and analysis on possible improvements to the feedback process. If you are able to, you could also arrange to observe each other and offer some analysis on the way each of you provides verbal feedback to individuals and and/or groups. (You could use the statements above as an observation guide.)
- Carry out a small piece of research to discover how your learners prefer to receive feedback on their work and progress. You could design a small set of questions for them to respond to or you could conduct a short whole group discussion that deals with a few set questions. Alternatively you could ask them to complete the following:

    - Feedback helps me to...
    - The best feedback shows me...
    - Feedback needs to be...
    - The most important thing about feedback is...
    - Sometimes feedback makes me feel...
    - The sort of feedback that motivates me most is...
    - I use feedback to...

Use the results from the research to draw up a feedback action plan for your group that employs the most appropriate suggestions and use it when teaching them. After a suitable period, you could evaluate the outcomes by comparing notes with a colleague and asking your learners for some feedback on your new approach.

Title of activity: Motivating learners

Domain links: A, B, C, D, E, F

Introduction

As teachers, we may often wish that our learners seemed more motivated to learn. Learning as a process can be tough and if you look at some of the theories of human motivation, particularly the humanistic ones, you will note the role that it is said to play in success. Think, for example, about extrinsic and intrinsic rewards and the part they play in promoting the level of drive and effort needed for many types of learning.

Extrinsic rewards come from outside the learner. They could take the form of a promotion, a qualification or a prize. One problem is that this form of motivation may encourage surface learning where the main goal is to get the reward rather than to learn or develop oneself. Surface learning also means that the learning is often forgotten once the goal is reached.

Intrinsic rewards, by contrast, emanate from the internal drives of the learner and are influenced quite often by previous experiences, either personal or vicarious, that have demonstrated the satisfaction to be gained from achievement through effort.

How do you spot those lacking in motivation? Look out for:

● time-wasting behaviour;
● avoidance of eye contact or turned-away posture;
● lack of initiative when working on an assignment or task;
● frequent calls for help but failure to take advice;
● reduced attention times and frequent distraction;
● absenteeism and arriving late for session;

- poor quality work and low participation in learning activities;
- losing, or forgetting to bring work to the session.

Development brief

Open a file for this activity.

- Do some background reading about motivation to remind yourself of the theories that underlie this important aspect of your practice.
- Summarise the main theories in your own words.
- Put together a case study that identifies and examines the main motivators as you see them, for a small cross-section of your current learners. It is best not to identify by name, those you are discussing, so either leave them anonymous or give them new names.
- For each person in your study, suggest at least three strategies you could take to harness their motivation and encourage them to achieve. Link your strategies to theories where you can.
- Put some of the most appropriate motivating strategies into practice in the learning environment and write a short reflective piece on the outcome.

REFLECTION

- The most important point I have discovered about motivation is that...
- When I notice poor motivation in any of my learners, three tactics I can instantly employ are...
- Both intrinsic and extrinsic motivators can work for learners because...
- The most useful bit of theory I read about said...
- Helping learners to be motivated will have an effect on their lives beyond the learning environment because...

Title of activity: Using experiential learning strategies

Domain links: A, B, C, D, F

Introduction

Experiential learning is often defined as 'learning by doing'. A learner could, for example, learn to follow a set of movements by copying their teacher. That would be imitation, though it would not necessary be experiential. This is because, for learning to be experiential, it would need to involve more complex behaviour that includes:

- thinking reflectively about the process of the doing;
- being able to abstract that thinking and learning and shift it to a different context where the same learning could be applied in a new situation.

If you think about your teacher training, much of it was probably set within a framework of reflective practice. It is likely that you were encouraged to write a reflective diary and by doing so, were being asked to explore the concrete experiences of your practice. Reflecting in this way would have helped you to extract the learning from an experience and by using your imagination, generalise that learning to new and different aspects of your professional life. (This is a bit like the function of the reflective prompts that come after each activity in this book.) Later, in a more practical sense, you would have been able to verify any generalisation you had made by testing it out in the learning environment and noting the outcome.

Development brief

Open a file for this activity.

- Identify a model of experiential learning and explain how it works in theory.
- In your own words and using a real example, show how the experiential model works for your learners in practice.
- Devise three strategies that encourage your learners to reflect on experience and generalise learning to new situations.

REFLECTION

- Looking at this theory in more detail has helped me to understand more about...
- I help my learners to maximise their learning from experience by...
- Teaching my learners new ways to think more reflectively should benefit them beyond the life of this course because...
- One aspect of experiential theory that I wish I understood better is...
- Experiential learning is an ongoing process for me as a practitioner because...

Title of activity: How effective is my management of learning?

Domain links: A, B, C, D, E, F

Introduction

Effective management of learning is not just about what you do in the learning environment when you are being a teacher or tutor. Much of your effectiveness could be said to be influenced by planning, preparation and post-learning evaluation too.

Development brief

Open a file for this activity. Carefully go through the statements below and write an honest and reflective response to each one.

- I always plan to include all my learners in the session by actively organising and managing participation.
- I am sensitive to issues around culture, ethnicity, gender and age and take account of them when planning and conducting teaching and learning.
- Through early diagnostic assessment, I am aware of individual learning needs and have strategies to manage them in my lesson plans.
- My planning gives me enough time to prepare good quality resources to meet a range of learning needs.
- I prepare the learning environment to maximise physical comfort and safety.
- Good planning allows me to differentiate learning tasks and activities so that everyone can meet their potential.
- I like to have high-quality visual material available to reinforce the verbal points I make.
- Every learning session has a range of group and individual tasks to help keep learners active.
- I always have a back-up plan and a few extra resources for when unexpected events occur.
- I network and negotiate to obtain support for learners who need it.
- I keep proper and consistent records of learner attendance and achievement.
- I positively encourage observers into my classes and welcome their feedback.
- I plan my marking in the same way that I plan my teaching so I can return work speedily.
- My marking is reliable and the feedback I give reflects standards that are known and understood by the learners.
- The reflection I do after each session helps me to plan and make necessary adjustments for the next one.

When you have written all your responses and you feel that they adequately reflect what you currently do on a regular basis, put aside some time to discuss each of them in turn with a trusted colleague or mentor.

- Select three aspects from the above list that you feel you already do particularly well and outline them. Identify the skills you demonstrate when carrying them out.
- Select three aspects that you could improve on and say why.
- Devise a simple strategy for each aspect that will allow you to demonstrate increased effectiveness in that area.
- Devise an action plan to implement your new strategies.
- Carry out your strategies over a period of time as discussed with your colleague and note the outcomes for you and your learners.

REFLECTION

- Carrying out this activity has made me feel...
- Discussing this with a colleague helped me to realise that...
- The impact on my learners of carrying out this activity has been...
- One other aspect not identified here that I wish to improve is...
- The next aspect I am planning to work on is...

Title of activity: Managing learner internet activity in my teaching sessions

Domain links: A, B, C, D, E

Introduction

To meet learning outcomes and syllabus requirements, learners often need to demonstrate their skills of searching and retrieving sources of information from the internet. This leads to all sorts of issues such as how you monitor and control what learners are doing and assess the quality of the information they are accessing and using. In a large group it may be very difficult to oversee every aspect of their internet behaviour, even if you wanted to. The most sensible approach might be to manage their learning behaviour more efficiently by some careful pre-planning when such sessions are due.

Below are some strategies you could introduce before the learners begin that could make learning with the internet more efficient and productive for them and more effectively managed by you.

- Be specific about what you want them to do and achieve before the end of the session. If you want them all to identify three sites or four pieces of information to present or discuss in 30 minutes time, say so. There is less likely to be unproductive behaviour if clear goals with timings are set.

- Emphasise that you expect proper referencing if they plan to use the material discovered in their own work later. It may be worth revisiting issues around attribution and plagiarism from time to time.

- You may want them all to visit a particular site. Check it out thoroughly yourself first if possible, so you are aware of any potential issues. Have the address available.

- Be clear about how much time they have to complete each stage of the activity and ask them to be responsible for the way they manage their time. Use countdown strategies to warn them how much time they have left for a task.

- Plan ahead so that you have a strategy in place to promote learning from the internet activity. Have a further task organised that will get them to outline, review and evaluate their findings or evaluate the quality of the site, for example.

- Consider asking them to work in pairs or small groups sometimes. This will encourage them to discuss their findings as they go along in anticipation of the review and evaluation.

- Ask them to clearly record or bookmark useful sites to share with others.

Development brief

Open a file for this activity.

- Write a short piece that outlines, as you see it, the main issues for teachers like you who have to manage aspects of internet behaviour as part of your teaching and learning responsibilities.

- Write a second piece that proposes some sensible strategies you could introduce to manage such situations as you describe above. Do any of your proposed strategies have a basis in learning theory?

- Write a third piece four to six weeks later that evaluates the strategies you introduced in terms of their outcomes for you and your learners.

Title of activity: Devising useful formative evaluation strategies to support my practice

Domain links: A, C, D, E

Introduction

Generally, a lot of emphasis is placed on the usefulness of the evaluation process as a tool for examining your practice. From a learner perspective, formative evaluation is potentially more to their advantage since you have an opportunity to adjust aspects of your practice with their specific feedback in mind as they progress through the course. Having said that learner feedback is critical, it remains the case that you will only achieve useful and valid outcomes if you gather the right data under the appropriate circumstances and then proceed to do something proactive with the results.

Gathering appropriate and more valid evaluation data can be done by:

- Being clear in your mind about what you want to know.
- Asking simple questions that are unambiguous and jargon-free.
- Including everyone in the process.
- Gathering the data at the appropriate times in the session and the course.
- Evaluating all aspects of the learner experience.
- Mixing the ways of acquiring evidence. Try using discussion or focus groups, questionnaires, group written and verbal feedback.
- Don't just go for tick-box responses. Ask for some real opinions and ideas.
- Avoid 'happy-sheet' syndrome, where the same generic form is handed out so regularly that the learners don't take the process seriously.
- Accepting all evidence as valid, even if it is uncomfortable.

- Combining learner feedback with achievement data if appropriate.
- Combining learner feedback with your own reflections and, if you can, the reflections of a colleague following and observation or discussion.

Having done the above, you can complete the process by:

- Reflecting on the responses you get and by doing so, devising sensible solutions to any issues.
- Feeding back to learners if appropriate.
- Acting to apply the solutions, adjustments or initiatives.
- Evaluating the outcomes of the new behaviours and re-calibrating if necessary.

The second element of formative evaluation that dovetails with the one above is the process by which you evaluate your own skills and abilities as a practitioner following every taught session. Some of you may faithfully complete an evaluation sheet after every session, others may jot down a few lines of post-session thoughts now and again or only when they have a problem. Many more do neither and are content to 'reflect' while dashing to the next timetabled task. Whichever way you go about it, the critical aspects of any valid self-evaluation are that they are conducted consistently using reflective thought and that any future actions arrived at through this process are applied and reviewed in the same spirit.

Development brief

Open a file for this activity.

- Carry out a case study to investigate the validity of the formative evaluation process as you usually conduct it in respect of a specific course you teach. You can use the bullet points above as a guide.
- Set up a new formative evaluation process for this case study and gather evidence via learner feedback at sensible intervals.
- Instigate a process of simple but reflective recorded self-evaluations that you can use regularly.
- Ask for a teaching observation and feedback from a colleague or use (with permission) one that has recently been completed.
- Process all the formative evaluation data at regular intervals by reflecting on the range of evidence you have, seeking guidance if needed and taking actions and reviewing changes as necessary.
- Summarise your case study and discuss the ways in which evaluation processes and reflective practice have been positively linked to improve specific aspects of your practice.

> **REFLECTION**
>
> ● This development activity has had a positive impact on my teaching because...
>
> ● Two of the most significant pieces of feedback I gathered told me...
>
> ● When I think of it in terms of evaluation, I take the term 'validity' to mean ...
>
> ● The most challenging part of this activity for me was...
>
> ● The most effective way to gather valid feedback from my learners proved to be...

Title of activity: Going on work experience in a non-teaching setting

Domain links: A, B, F

Introduction

You may wonder about the value of this activity but there is much that can be learned from the experience of working in a completely different environment now and again. To begin with, a new environment tends to put all your senses on alert and you will find that you are probably much more observant and curious than might be the case in your everyday role. Try to secure some work-experience time – a week tends to be the minimum that is useful – and be adventurous about your choice. If you are not the adventurous type, at least go for a lateral choice that will stimulate you and provide insights into working practices you are less familiar with. While you are there, keeping a reflective journal that comments on your experiences and what you can learn from them would be a good strategy. You could address the following as part of the reflective process.

● Why you selected this particular work experience. What were the features that drew you to it?

● How your role in this setting differs from your usual one and how you feel about that.

● The extent to which new or less-used talents and skills are asked of you and how you feel about that.

● What is it about the venue and facilities that feel different? Are there things you miss? Are there facilities at the work experience that would be good to have in your real workplace?

● Examine the people-based practices. How do they communicate, manage tasks, organise themselves, network? How do those practices compare with those you are usually involved in?

- How much control do individual workers have over the way they manage their everyday roles and responsibilities compared to you in your usual role?
- How is your view of the world and the way it operates affected by the job you do and the employer you work for?
- What were you able to give to the process?
- What did you gain from the process?
- How might the experience be useful to your role as a practitioner?

Development brief

Open a file for this activity.

- Arrange a work experience placement for yourself at a time that is convenient to you and your employer.
- Attend the placement with the aim of immersing yourself in the new environment.
- Be anthropological. Be curious, ask questions, join in rather than merely observe, reflect on events and write them down regularly. What is new? What are you learning? Look at the how and the why of the differences you are experiencing and reflect on how the most useful elements could be adapted to your practice.
- Future-pace the introduction of some useful elements gathered from work experience. This means simply imagining how you could effectively integrate some of the most valuable aspects of your experience into your practice.
- Produce a means of communicating your experiences and reflections on the whole process. It could be a video or photo diary, a more conventional written reflective diary or even an audio diary. The key is to really reflect on what can be learned by the experience about yourself and the relationship you have with the wider world.

REFLECTION

- If a colleague was planning to undergo some work experience I would advise them to...
- The most interesting aspect of this activity was...
- My role as a practitioner links to and has an impact on the world of work because...
- The most useful element I have drawn from my work experience to implement in practice is...
- When I returned to my practitioner role, I felt...

Title of activity: Shadowing to develop new roles and responsibilities

Domain links: A, B

Introduction

One of the best ways to develop the skills needed to take on new roles and responsibilities is to 'shadow', officially or unofficially, the person currently in the post or carrying out the role. If you have always wanted to be a personal tutor, teach your subject to entirely different groups, manage a team or be a mentor, for example, shadowing will provide you with the information and insight with which to make an informed decision about what to aim for. Clearly, the first step here would be to get consent from your line manager and the person you intend to shadow. Shadowing is not about trying to usurp someone's position. It is about gaining insight into the skill-sets needed to carry out the role properly and obtaining the support to develop those abilities with a view to progressing your career. Once you have obtained the permission and are shadowing a role, you can reflect and comment on the following.

- What does the shadow role entail that is different from your current one?
- What is it about the role that motivates you personally and professionally?
- What skills does the shadow role need that you already possess?
- What skills does the shadow role need that you would have to develop?
- How would the shadow role fit in with your current responsibilities?
- What level of commitment would you need to make to take on the role in terms of time?

Development brief

Open a file for this activity.

- Address the questions above carefully for your file.
- Arrange to shadow the role you have selected, ensuring first that you have the necessary permissions before proceeding.
- Keep a reflective journal that charts your shadow experience over a period of time, noting the development of your skills and evaluating the insights into the role gained by the process.

Title of activity: Single or mutual peer observation in the learning environment

Domain links: A, B, C, D, E

Introduction

There is potentially a lot to learn from peer observation, particularly if you follow the reflect–observe–reflect–discuss–reflect approach. You may wonder what the value is of observing someone who has the same level of experience as you do. The value is in the process of collaboration and mutual development through observation and reflection. It is also quite possible that your colleague approaches teaching in a different way to you, employs other strategies to promote learning and specialises in a different subject area. This last point is important. It is not necessary to observe someone who teaches the same subject as you do unless you are doing this activity to observe the way specialist subject knowledge and resources are deployed. In fact some practitioners argue that it is useful to observe someone teaching something you are less familiar with because you then find it easier to concentrate on their teaching skills alone. Remember too, that the philosophy behind this activity is to develop your skills, particularly your teaching skills, but also your skills of reflection, observation, interpretation and diplomacy. If you are concerned about selecting the most appropriate criteria for any observation, there is a wide range of criteria relating to effective teaching and learning strategies outlined in many of the activities in Chapter 5 that should help you.

Development brief

Open a file for this activity.

- Design an observation document that includes the sort of criteria outlined in many of the activities in Chapter 5. Reflect on and include any other criteria that you feel are important for your development.
- Arrange observation times with a peer/colleague.

- Attend observations for a minimum of one hour and take notes to address the criteria. Notes are better than tick-box responses since they are more likely to aid reflection later.
- After the observation spend some time reflecting on what you saw, using your notes, your experience and education theory knowledge to support you. Make further notes if you plan to raise points at the feedback.
- Meet to engage with feedback and discussion. This may be mutual if you agreed to observe each other. Ensure that your feedback is objective, constructive and supportive. If you have any concerns about what you observe it may be best to ask questions rather that voice criticisms. 'What do you think, in hindsight, would have been the best thing to do in that case?' certainly sounds better than 'I think you got that all wrong, didn't you?'
- Write up your observations, how you gave and/or received feedback, together with reflections on the process as a whole and what has been achieved by participating in the activity.
- Finish by identifying three positive outcomes for your practice of participating in this activity.

REFLECTION

- Two ideas I could adapt from the observation and use with my own learners would be...
- Feedback on my teaching observation suggests that...
- The part of this activity I found the most challenging was...
- On reflection, this activity should have a positive impact on my teaching because...
- My skills of collaboration, peer observation and feedback and mutual reflection were...

Title of activity: Observe an experienced practitioner

Domain links: A, B, C, D, E

Introduction

If you opt for this activity, make your selection of person to observe with care. Experience is not necessarily a guarantee of model practitioner behaviour. It is not essential and probably not possible to locate perfection but it is in your interest to observe someone that you respect, such as a mentor, rather than go for someone because they are available at a time you are free.

- The main aim of this activity is to draw out the characteristics of practitioner experience and identify how certain skills and behaviours that you observe can be modelled by you and used to advantage in your own practice.
- A secondary aim is to put yourself in the situation of the observed practitioner and reflect on the choices they made and say if you might have done anything differently in the same situation.

When designing your observation criteria, remember the most effective tools for this purpose usually include an evaluation of:

- the pre-session planning in terms of a scheme of work and lesson plan that identify properly stated aims and desired learning outcomes;
- the organisation of the learning environment to ensure, physical and emotional comfort and safety for learners;
- the organisation and management of resources to support learner needs;
- the deployment of a suitable and varied assortment of learning strategies;
- the deployment of a suitable and varied assortment of valid and reliable assessment strategies;
- effective management of the learning process throughout the session;
- the way the session is brought to a close to ensure learning is retained and linked to the next session.

Development brief

Open a file for this activity.

- Organise the assessment criteria you plan to use when you are observing (see above for some ideas about what to include).
- Identify the person you wish to observe as an experienced practitioner and approach them to arrange a suitable date and time.
- Explain the purpose of the exercise to them and agree issues of confidentiality and/or anonymity in your written report as appropriate.
- Attend the observation, ensuring the minimum of disruption to the session.
- Reflect and write up your evaluation. What you gain from this process could be some valuable insights and inspiring ideas. Equally you may have some more sobering reflections that compel you to question what you have seen in terms of theory or your own practice knowledge. Remember that even learning how not to do something is developmental if you reflect on it properly.
- Thank the person you observed for their co-operation and offer to meet with them if they would like any feedback.
- If you do provide feedback, either written or verbal, be professional and objective. Concentrate on clarification rather than criticism. Ask questions rather than pronounce judgements.

Title of activity: Setting and keeping ground rules with learners

Domain links: A, C, D, E, F

Introduction

When you meet with a learning group for the first time it is helpful to promote cohesion and participation from the outset. One strategy that can increase learner confidence and support emotional safety is to work with your learners to identify a set of ground rules that meet the needs of everyone, including you.

Development brief

Open a file for this activity.

- Select one or more groups to work with. If you decide to carry out this activity with more than one group, you could later compare responses across age groups or courses.
- As near to the beginning of a course as you can, ask the group as a whole to define what they think ground rules are and why they might be important to the manner in which the group develops.

Your discussion might include the following.

- Ground rules are about how the group should behave.
- Ground rules are about how the group and the teacher should behave.
- Ground rules are a waste of time because no one keeps to them.
- Ground rules are effective because when everyone has set and agreed them, they are harder to break.
- They are helpful because people like to know what is expected of them.
- They should be decided by the tutor.

- They should be decided by the learners.
- They should be decided by everyone involved.
- Ground rules should be reasonable and fair.
- If you have ground rules, what do the group want to do when someone breaks one of them?
- If there are too many rules, people will forget what they are.

Once you have had a discussion to identify factors such as those shown above, you could do the following.

- You could ask them to work in small groups to decide some of the ground rules they would like to see adopted on their course. This may need more time than you would think since people often disagree about rules and how they should be applied, so remind them that they are deciding rules to be kept in practice that need to be agreed by all.
- Once that is done you will need to briefly discuss each suggestion in terms of application. It is interesting how draconian rules devised this way can often sound, so you may need to point out issues such as exceptional circumstances, individual differences that need to be respected and special cases that will require more thought before the wording is appropriate.
- Once the ground rules are agreed (by you and the group) someone should type them up and either produce a copy for everyone or produce one large copy for the learning venue.
- When you write up your notes for this activity, you can evaluate the effectiveness, or otherwise, of establishing ground rules this way as opposed to imposing them on your learners.
- If you wish to add an extra professional dimension to this activity, there is some theory that you could explore that connects andragogy and pedagogy to the processes of managing adult learning.

REFLECTION

- Establishing ground rules meets a number of the emotional needs of my learners because...
- When devising and agreeing the rules my learners also gained insight into...
- If there were no rules at all for this course the outcome might be...
- The difference between andragogy and pedagogy in terms of ground rules and the way they could be applied would be...
- My professional opinion about ground-rules and their application in the learning environment is...

Appendix

List of development activities

Professional values, professional behaviour, specialist knowledge and pedagogy

Planning, delivering, assessing and supporting learning

References and further reading

Bandura, A. (1977) *Social learning theory*. New York: General Learning Press.

Belbin, R.M. (1996) *Team roles at work*. Oxford: Butterworth and Heinemann.

Brookfield, S.D. (1995) *Becoming critically reflective teachers*. San Francisco: Jossey-Bass.

DfES (2006) *Further education: Raising skills, improving life chances*. Government White Paper. London: HMSO.

Flanagan, J.C. (1954) The critical incident technique. *Psychological Bulletin*, 51 (4): 327–358.

Grinder, J. and Bandler, R. (1976) *The struture of magic 2*. Palo Alto: Science and Behaviour Books.

Hillier, Y. (2002) *Reflective teaching in further and adult education*. London: Continuum.

Peters, J.M. (1994) Instructors as researcher and theorists: Faculty development in a community college, in R. Benn and R. Fieldhouse (eds) *Training and professional development in adult and continuing education*. Exeter: CRCE.

Schön, D. (1987) *Educating the reflective practitioner: Towards a new design for teaching and learning in the professions*. San Francisco: Jossey-Bass.

Tuckman, B.W. and Jensen, M.A.C. (1977) Stages of small group development revisited. *Group and Organisational Studies* 2: 419–427.

You may find the following websites useful, though their addresses, content and mission may alter over time.

Association of Colleges
www.aoc.co.uk

Adult Learning Inspectorate
www.ali.gov.uk

Basic Skills Agency
www.basic-skills.co.uk

British Dyslexia Association
www.bdadyslexia.org.uk

British Educational Research Association
www.bera.ac.uk

City and Guilds
www.cityandguilds.org.uk

Chartered Institute of Personnel and Development
www.cipd.co.uk

Copyright Licensing Agency
www.cla.org.uk

Education Resource Information Centre
www.eric.ed.gov/

Further Education Regional Research Network
www.sfeu.ac.uk

Institute for Learning
www.ifl.ac.uk

Intute (formerly the Social Science Information Gateway: sosig)
www.intute.ac.uk

JANET. Education and research network.
www.ja.net

Learning and Skills Council
www.lsc.gov.uk

Learning and Skills Development Agency
www.lsda.org.net

Learning and Skills Network
www.lsneducation.org.uk

Lifelong Learning UK
www.lluk.org.uk

National Institute for Adult Continuing Education
www.niace.org.uk

National Foundation for Educational Research
www.nfer.ac.uk

Qualifications and Curriculum Authority (QCA)
www.qca.org.uk

Quality Assurance Agency (QAA)
www.qaa.ac.uk

University for Industry
www.ufi.com